<경제 이론과 현실> 제4권, 완결편 개정판

연구방법론

Methodology of Economics

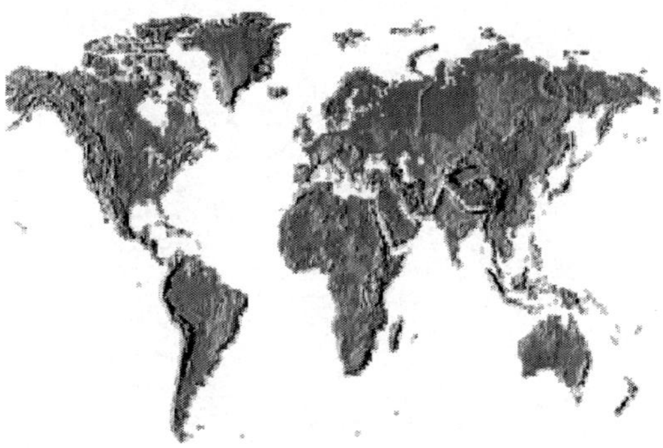

세 계 경 제 문 제 연 구 소

이 책 시리즈 1, 2, 3, 4권을 세트발행(동시발행)하기전에, 이에 적합하도록 입증자료로서 중요한 의미가 있는 것은 각각의 입증자료의 이면여백에 그 의미를 요약 설명하였으며, 교정도 하였다. 그리고 세트발행의 편의상 입증자료의 말미에 "자연실업률의 측정상의 문제"를 "디스인플레이션과 자연률 이론"으로 내용을 교체하여 이 책을 개정판으로 세트발행하고자 하였다.

2015년 4월 10일

정 기 옥

서 언

후진국의 외환위기에 대해서는 경제학자들마다 연구방법과 내용이 다르기 때문에 이를 체계적으로 연구하는 방법론은 경제모델의 설정의 문제가 아니라 모델의 선택과 평가의 문제일 수 밖에 없다. 이와 같은 방법론은 우리경제의 현실을 설명하는데 적합할 뿐만 아니라 세계적으로 유명한 경제학자들의 여러이론을 소개하고 입증하는 방법으로서도 유용하였다. 이 책은 이와 같은 목적을 다하기 위해서 2006년과 2007년 「학술원」에 "경제이론과 현실" 평가용으로 제출했던 두 개의 팜플렛을 하나로 엮어 책으로 만든 것이다.

하버드 대학 교수의 책을 비판해야만 우리경제의 현실을 설명할 수 있고, 프린스턴 대학 교수의 책(2006년 초판)의 내용을 수정해야만 그 방법론을 입증할 수 있었듯이, 돌이켜 볼 때 거시경제와 국제금융론을 거시경제의 수요측면에서 통합하고 현실을 설명하는 책을 출판한다는 것은 참으로 어려운 일이었고 위험한 일이었다. 정치·사회적으로 혼란한 시기에 오해를 받을 소지가 많았기 때문이었다. 책에서 보듯이 이 책은 이론에 충실하고 있기 때문에 오해가 있을 수 없을 것으로 지금도 믿고 있다.

일본의 디플레이션 문제는 이 책의 제2권 「거시경제」 편에서 요약해서 설명한 바 있지만 이번기회에 입증자료에서 보다 자세하게 소개하고 있다. 이는 앞으로도 우리경제의 현실을 설명하는 데 유용하게 이용할 수 있을 것으로 생각한다.

1997년의 외환위기는 저량의 측면에서 보면 외채위기였으나 유량의 측면에서 보면 인플레이션에 의해서 환율이 장기적으로 조정이 되지 않았기 때문이었다. 이렇게 본다면 유량의 측면에서 본 환율위기는 2006년 5월부터 시작되어 2007년 11월 1일 현재까지도 지속되고 있다고 할 수 있다. 다만 외환위기 이후에 우리 경제의 생산성이 외국에 비해서 대폭적으로 향상되어 원·달러의 적정환율이 920원대라고 한다면 환율위기라고 할 수는 없을 것이다.

외환위기에 관한한 가능한 범위내에서 많은 경제학자들의 연구방법론과 내용이 소개되고 있기 때문에 이 책의 「시리즈」는 앞으로도 우리 경제의 현실을 설명하는데 유용한 자료가 될 수 있을 것으로 생각하고 있다. 특히 세계경제적인 측면에서 검증되고 입증되고 있기 때문에 세계의 주요국가의 현실을 설명하는 데에도 활용할 수 있을 것으로 보고 있다.

「경제이론과 현실」을 검증하고 입증하는 과정에서 가장 어려웠던 점이 경제학과 경영학과의 관계를 어떻게 정립할 것인가하는 문제였다. 예를 들면 "코스피지수(종합주가지수)가 2,000수준에서도 주가는 저평가되어있고 따라서 앞으로 1년후에 3,000까지 갈 수도 있으며, 우리경제는 매우 낙관적이어서 앞으로 10년동안 매년 7%의 성장도 가능하기 때문에 곧 선진국이 될 수 있다"라고 하는 말은 경영학적인 측면에서 본 매우 낙관적인 예측이라고 할 수 있다. 왜냐하면 경제학적인 측면에서 볼 때는, 개방경제의 거시경제적 현실은 아직도 거꾸로 가고 있으며, 환율위기는 아직도 지속되고 있다고 할 수 있기 때문이다. 자본주의 사회에서는 경제학이 기초학문인 이상 경영학은 경제학을 기초로 해야 하는 것은 아닐는지 학제간 연구가 필요한 시점이다. 이 책은 이와 같은 학제간 연구에도 도움이 될 수 있을 것으로 믿고 있다.

끝으로 그 동안 관계기관과 연구기관 및 언론기관에 여러 가지로 상충되는 점이 많아 송구스럽고, 고향의 친인척 및 선·후배님들에게 사회적인 책임을 다하지 못하여 죄송스러우며, 정형문, 정우문, 정소영이에게 아버지로서의 몫을 다하지 못하여 미안하게 생각한다. 머지않은 미래에 지금의 경제적 난국을 원만하게 해결해서 선진국으로 성장할 수 있기를 기대하고, 내년에는 이 책이 학계에서 인정되어 학문을 지속할 수 있게 되기를 기도하면서, 이로서 이 책의 서언에 대신하고자 한다.

2007년 11월 1일

정 기 옥

경제모델의 평가방법, PP.3-16

입증자료(영문), PP.17-171

세계경제문제 연구소

<경제 이론과 현실>연구방법론

경제모델(Economic model)의 평가 방법

Evaluation of a model

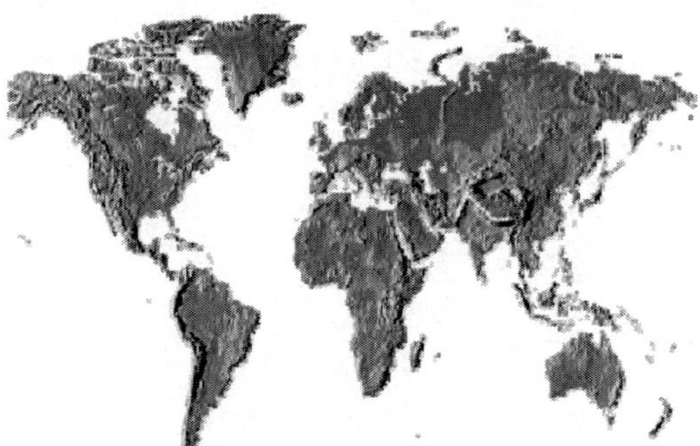

세계경제문제연구소

목 차

1. 서 론

1973년 노벨경제학상을 수상한 레온티에프(Leontief)는 미국의 통계자료를 이용하여 당시의 국제무역론(헥셔·오린 모델)을 검증하였는데, 통계자료로는 헥셔·오린모델(Heckscher Ohlin model)을 검증할 수 없었다. 그 후 모델자체의 가정과 가정으로부터 유도된 결론의 논리적 타당성 여·부에 대한 많은 검증이 이루어지면서, 국제무역론이 이론적으로 발전을 거듭하여 오늘에 이르고 있다.

똑같은 이유 때문에 먼델·플레밍모델(Mundell-Fleming model)을 우리가 받아들이기 위해서는 이를 검증하고 평가할 필요성이 있다. 먼델·플레밍 모델은 개방경제의 거시이론의 일반론이다. 그러나 이는 미국을 중심으로 한 선진국에서 검증된 이론이기 때문에 우리경제의 입장에서 모델의 타당성(적합성) 여·부를 검증하고 난 다음에야 이를 이용할 수 있게 된다. 미국에서 개발되고 선진국에서 검증된 경제적 모델(economic model)이 모든 국가에서 타당하지 않을 수도 있기 때문이다.

먼델·플레밍 모델을 통계적으로 검증할 수 없다고 해서 이를 부정할 수는 없기 때문에 우리의 입장에서 어떻게 보완할 것인가하는 문제가 무엇보다도 중요한 과제일 수 밖에 없다. 통계적으로 검증할 수 없는 경우에 이론적으로 검증이 필요한 이유가 여기에 있다. 그러기 위해서는 거시경제의 수요측면에서 통합하고 국제금융론의 측면에서 검증되어야만 한다. 왜냐하면 국제수지와 외환시장 및 환율제도상의 문제 또한 중요하기 때문이다.

외국에서 개발되고 외국에서 검증된 경제모델을 우리 경제의 입장에서 검증하는 것은 「경제이론과 현실」의 연구 방법론일 수 밖에 없다. 왜냐하면 기존의 외국의 책과는 다른 책이 될 수 밖에 없기 때문이다. 특히 이 책은 세계경제적인 측면에서 검증되고 있기 때문에 다른 국가의 경제현실을 설명하는 연구방법으로도 활용할 수 있을 것으로 생각한다.

경제모델의 검증방법과 관련해서 아직까지도 중요하게 논의되는 것이 위에서 말한 레온티에프의 역설이다. 왜냐하면 통계상의 문제가 아니라 논리적(이론적)인 문제이기 때문이다. 따라서 레온티에프 역설(Leontief paradox)은 먼델·플레밍 모델의 검증방법을 보완하는 자료로 유용하게 이용할 수 있다. 뿐만 아니라 헥셔·오린모델과 먼델플레밍 모델은 국제경제학의 가장 기본적인 모델이기 때문에 이 두 모델의 검증방법은 미시·거시·국제경제이론을 종합적으로 분석하여 현실을 설명하는데 유용한 연구방법론으로 활용할 수 있다. 이 팜플렛은 「경제이론과 현실」의 내용이 너무 방대하기 때문에 그 방법론을 심사용으로 작성한 것이다.

2006년 4월

정 기 옥

2. 경제학의 연구방법론

모든 과학의 목적은 현실(현상)을 설명하는데 있다. 경제학(경제이론)도 경제적 현상(경제적 현실)을 설명하는데 그 목적이 있다고 할 수 있는데 현실경제는 매우 복잡하기 때문에 이를 단순화시킬 필요성이 있다. 복잡한 현실경제를 단순화하기 위해서는 가정을 설정해야만 한다. 예를들어 단순한 시장경제 모델에서 "정부가 존재하지 않는다면"은 가정의 설정이고 이와같은 가정의 설정으로부터 정부가 존재하지 않는 단순한 시장경제 모델이 성립된다. "과잉공급이나 초과수요가 존재한다면"은 원인이고 "균형가격이 성립할때까지 가격은 상승하거나 하락할 것이다."는 결과이다. 따라서 경제모델(economic model)은 인과관계를 유도하기 위해서 복잡한 경제현실을 단순화시킨 이론적 모형이라고 할 수 있다.

현실경제가 복잡한 이유는 현실경제를 결정하는 요인이 복잡하기 때문이다. 위의 예에서 가격이외에 수요와 공급을 결정하는 다른 요인이 일정한 경우에만 인과관계인 균형가격이 결정되는 과정을 설명할 수 있게 된다. "다른 요인이 일정하다면"이라는 여건불변의 가정은 경제이론 또는 모델이 많은 가정으로 구성되어 있기 때문이다.

가정의 설정으로부터 성립된 경제적 모델은 어느시기, 어떤 국가에서도 타당한 경제이론이 될 수 있는지 또는 그렇지 않은지 검증할 필요성이 있다. 바꾸어 말한다면 시간과 장소를 초월해서 타당한 이론이 될 수 있는지 그 여부를 검증해야만 한다는 것이다.

예를들면 미국이나 선진국에서 타당한 경제이론이 우리의 입장에서는 타당하지 않을 수도 있고, 1970년대에는 인과관계에 모순이 없었던 경제이론이 오늘의 시대에는 모순이 되는 결과가 발생해서 하나의 경제이론으로 받아들일 수 없는 경우도 있을 수 있을 것이다. 이와같은 경우에는 기존의 모델을 보완하거나, 새로운 모델을 연구해서 도입할 필요성이 있게 된다.

미시, 거시이론에서 소개되는 경제이론 또는 모델들은 이미 검증된 이론들이기 때문에 일반적으로는 검증할 필요성이 없다고 할 수 있다. 그러나 최근에야 일반이론이 된 국제금융론에서의 먼델·플레밍모델(Mundell-Fleming model)은 우리경제의 입장에서 검증되어야만 한다. 왜냐하면 최근에야 일반이론이 되었을 뿐만 아니라 미국이나 선진국에서 검증된 이론으로 우리의 입장에서는 여러 측면에서 결함이 있기 때문이다.

검증은 가정을 검증하는 것이 아니라 인과관계가 보편적인 원칙이 될 수 있는가 하는 모델의 설명능력에 따라서 검증된다. 따라서 경제적 모델은 일반적으로 통계에 의해서 검증된다. 왜냐하면 통계자체가 보편적인 원칙이 반영된 현실을 반영하는 것이기 때문이다. 그러나 통계적으로는 검증이 될 수 없는 경제적 모델이 있을 수 있다. 왜냐하면 인과관계에 모순이 있을 수도 있고 가정자체에 문제가 있을 수도 있기 때문이다. 이와같은 경우에는 이론적인 검증이 필요하다.

먼델·플레밍모델이 통계적으로는 검증이 안되는 이유가 위와 같은 이유때문이다. 미국에서는 "정부(중앙은행)가 외환시장에 개입하지 않는다면"이라는 가정에서 통계적 검증이 가능하지만 우리의 입장에서는 통계적으로 먼델·플레밍모델을 검증할 수 없기 때문이다. 이에 대한 내용은 3절에서 구체적으로 설명되고 있다.

먼델·플레밍모델의 검증방법은 레온티에프의 역설 이후 헥셔·오린 모델을 검증했던 방법론을 참고하였다. 이에 대한 내용은 4절에서 구체적으로 설명되고 있다. 그리고 선진국에서 이미 검증된 모델을 우리경제의 입장에서 재검증하는 것이므로 본문에서는 "응용"이라는 용어를 사용했었으나 이번 기회에 이를 "검증"이라는 용어로 통일시키고자 하였다.

우리경제의 입장에서 어떤 경제모델을 검증한다는 것은 선진국에서 검증된 경제모델이 우리경제의 현실적인 측면에서 볼 때 중요한 결함이 있어 이를 보완할 목적으로 재검증한다는 뜻이다. 이는 현실을 설명하기 위한 연구방법론이라고 할 수 있다. 「경제이론과 현실」의 연구방법론으로 먼델·플레밍모델을 우리 경제의 입장에서 재검증하였고, 부족한 것은 미국에서 이미 검증해서 널리 알려진 헥셔·오린 모델 검증결과로 보완하였다.

3. 먼델·플레밍모델(Mundell-Fleming model)의 검증방법

먼델·플레밍모델을 검증하고 이를 평가하기 위해서는 이론적으로 거시경제와 국제금융론이 통합이 되어야만 한다. 거시경제와 국제금융론은 국제금융론의 측면에서도 통합이 가능하다. 그러나 국제금융론의 측면에서 통합하면 거시경제적 현실을 설명하기가 어렵기 때문에 현실을 설명하기 위해서는 거시경제의 수요측면에서 통합이 되어야만 한다.

거시경제의 수요측면에서 통합하는 방법은 수식으로 통합하든가 아니면 이론적으로 통합되어야만 한다. 수식으로 통합하는 방법은 국제금융론의 변수를 도입해서 통합하는 방법이다. 예를들면 국가위험성(country risk)과 예상환율이라는 변수를 추가하는 것이 그 것이다. 그러나 이와 같은 변수이외에 다른 중요한 국제금융론상의 문제들은 설명이 될 수 없기 때문에 먼델·플레밍모델을 검증하고 평가해서 현실을 설명하는데 문제가 있다. 이에 대한 구체적인 내용은 입증자료에서 자세히 설명되고 있다.

따라서 이 모델을 받아들이기 위해서는 이 모델의 가정에 문제가 있는지 없는지 검토해야 한다. 이 모델의 기본적인 가정은 "정부(중앙은행)가 외환시장에 개입하지 않는다면"이라는 가정이다. 그렇다면 정부가 외환시장에 개입하는 우리경제의 입장에서는 가정상의 일관성의 문제를 어떻게 처리해야 하는가? 정부가 외환시장에 개입하지 않는 단순한 외환시장 모델을 도입하면 정부(중앙은행)가 외환시장에 개입하지 않는 경우와 개입하는 경우를 비교평가 할 수 있다. 즉 중앙은행(한국은행)이 외환시장에 개입하지 않는다고 가정한다면 가정의 일관성을 유지 할 수 있다. 이는 단순한 외환시장 모델에 의해서도 먼델·플레밍모델을 평가 할 수 있다는 뜻이다.

이렇게해서 통합이 되면 국제수지문제와 외환위기 문제뿐만 아니라 먼델·플레밍모델을 어떻게 평가하고 받아들일 것인가하는 문제를 설명할 수 있다. 이론을 단순화하기 위해서 2006년 3월의 외환보유고도 적정수준이 되었고, 환율도 상호무역이 될 수 있는 적정환율 범위에서 안정적으로 변동하고 있다고 가정하자. 그러면 먼델·플레밍모델을 따를 수 밖에 없을 것이다. 왜냐하면 이 이론은 일반론일 뿐만아니라 우리 경제의 거시경제적인 현실을 설명할 수 있는 모델이기 때문이다.

먼델·플레밍모델을 받아들일 수 밖에 없는 이유가 여기에 있다. 이 이론은 세계적인 일반론이기 때문에 이를 부정할 수가 없다는 점에서도 중요하지만, 더욱더 중요한 것은 이 이론을 받아들여야 거시경제적 현실을 설명할 수 있다는 것이다. 이유는 이 이론이 IS-LM분석을 기초로 하고 있기 때문이다.

지금까지 설명은 거시경제적인 현실성의 측면에서 먼델·플레밍모델의 적합성을 설명한 것이다. 국제금융론의 측면에서 적합성에 대한 평가는 「경제이론과 현실」 종결편에서 충분하게 설명이 되었기 때문에 더 이상의 설명이 필요없을 것이다. 그 외에도 이 이론은 단순한 시장경제모델을 전제로 하고 있기 때문에 시장구조론과도 모순이 없이 부합된다고 할 수 있다.

요약한다면 먼델·플레밍모델은 미시·거시·국제경제적인 측면에서 볼때 받아들일 수 밖에 없는 이론이라고 할 수 있다. 다만 아직까지는 우리경제의 대부자금시장(자본시장)이 이 이론을 받아들일 수 있을만큼 충분히 성숙(조성)되어 있지 않다고 할 수 있을 것이다. 예를들면 외국인의 국내주식투자의 증가로 자본이 유입되었을 때, 환율이 하락하고, 부동산투자수요의 증가로 부동산가격이 과도하게 상승할 수도 있을 것이다. 이와 같은 경우에도 환율이 적정수준이 될 수 있도록 자본의 유입을 통제하거나 부동산투자수요를 억제할 수 있는 방법이 있을 수 있다. 이에 대한 구체적인 내용은 입증자료에서 자세히 설명되고 있다.

지금까지 설명한 것을 요약한다면 거시경제의 수요측면에서 통합해야 개방경제의 거시경제적 현실을 설명할 수 있고, 국제금융론의 측면에서 검증되어야 먼델·플레밍모델의 적합성 여부를 검증할 수 있다는 것이다. 이에 대해서는 「경제이론과 현실」의 제 2권 "거시경제"와 "종결편"에 보다 더 자세하게 설명되어 있다. 여기에서 설명된 것은 방법론상의 측면에서 요약한 것에 지나지 않는다.

4. 레온티에프의 역설(Leontief paradox)

국제 경제적 모델은 국가간의 무역과 금융거래(자본거래)를 분석하는 모델이기 때문에 모델의 가정이 매우 복잡한 것이 특징이다. 따라서 모델의 가정과 가정으로부터 유도된 결론의 논리적 타당성에 문제가 있어 모델의 통계적 검증이 불가능한 경우가 있고 논란의 대상이 된다는 점에 그 특징이 있다. 대표적인 경우가 레온티에프의 역설이다.

이미 설명한 바와같이 1973년에 노벨경제학상을 수상한 레온티에프(Leontief)는 미국의 통계자료를 이용하여 당시의 국제무역론(헥셔·오린모델)을 검증하였는데, 헥셔·오린모델의 결론과는 반대되는 결과를 얻게 되었기 때문에 이를 레온티에프의 역설이라 한다. 그렇다면 레온티에프의 검증이 왜 역설이 되었는가? 그 중요한 이유는 지금도 그렇지만 헥셔·오린모델이 일반론이기 때문이다. 더욱더 중요한 것은 헥셔·오린모델이 "비용이 증가하는 생산가능곡선"을 전제로 하기 때문이다.

비용이 증가하는 생산가능곡선은 단순한 시장경제모델과 더불어 경제학에서 가장 기본적인 모델에 속한다. 생산의 효율성과 일반균형이론은 이 모델을 전제로 한 것이다. 따라서 헥셔·오린모델을 부정하는 것은 미시경제학 자체를 부정하는 것이 될 수밖에 없기 때문에 레온티에프의 검증이 역설로 남을 수 밖에 없게 된 것이다.

레온티에프의 역설을 먼델·플레밍모델의 검증방법과 관련해서 보완자료로 활용하기 위해서는 헥셔·오린모델(Heckscher-Ohlin model)의 가정을 검토해야한다. 헥셔·오린모델의 가정을 요약하면 다음과 같다.

1) 두 국가, 두 상품, 두 생산요소만이 존재한다.
이와같은 단순한 모델로부터 얻을수 있는 결론은 다수의 국가, 다수의 상품, 다수의 생산요소가 존재하는 현실경제에도 그대로 적용될 수 있다.

2) 양국의 생산물시장과 생산요소시장은 모두 완전경쟁시장이다.
당연한 결과로서 가격은 한계비용과 일치하고, 실업이 존재하지 않는다.

3) 양국의 선호와 취미는 동일하며 따라서 사회적 부차별 곡선도 동일하다.
국가간 선호와 취미는 다를수도 있는데 수요조건이 다른 경우에도 무역이 발생할 수 있다.

4) 수송비가 없고, 관세나 비관세 장벽이 존재하지 않는다.
따라서 국제무역론의 주요연구과제는 자유무역이며, 보호무역은 무역정책론에 속한다.

5) 양국의 자원(생산요소)과 기술수준은 주어져 있어 불변이다.
따라서 주어진 생산가능곡선상에서의 효율적인 자원배분 문제가 헥셔·오린모델의 주요 연구과제이다.

6) 양국의 기술수준은 동일하다.

양국의 생산함수가 동일할뿐만 아니라 기술 격차도 존재하지 않는다는 것이다.

7) 규모에 대한 보수는 불변이다.

이는 완전경쟁시장을 전제로 하기 때문에 규모의 경제가 존재하지 않는다는 뜻이다.

8) 상품간의 요소집약도는 역전되지 않는다.

예를들어 X재가 Y재보다 자본집약적인 상품이라면 어떠한 요소가격비에서도 이와 같은 요소집약도의 순위는 바뀌지 않는다는 것이다.

이상과 같은 가정하에서는 "미국은 자본이 풍부한 국가이므로 자본집약적인 상품을 수출하고 노동집약적인 상품을 수입한다."는 것이 헥셔·오린모델의 결론이다. 따라서 통계적으로 검증해도 이와같은 결론을 얻을 수 있어야 한다. 만약 이와같은 결론을 얻을 수 없을 경우에는 통계가 잘못되었거나 모델이 잘못되었다고 생각할 수 있을 것이다.

통계상에는 문제가 없었으므로 모델을 검증하여 타당성(적합성) 여부를 평가할 필요가 있었다. 바꾸어 말한다면 미국의 통계로는 헥셔·오린모델을 검증할 수 없었기 때문에 모델 자체의 적합성 여부를 검증해야만 한다는 것이다. 그 후의 모델의 검증결과를 요약한다면 다음과 같다.

1) 미국은 타국에 비해서 기술수준이 높기 때문에 자본과 기술노동집약적 상품(또는 인적자본 집약적 상품)을 수출하고, 자본과 단순노동집약적인 상품을 수입한다는 것이다. 따라서 노동을 동질적이라고 가정하는 것에 문제가 있다.
2) 미국은 자본을 많이 사용하는 자연자원집약적인 상품을 수입하므로 생산요소를 노동과 자본으로 구분하는 2요소모델(two factor model)에 문제가 있다.
3) 요소 집약도는 요소가격비에 따라 역전될 수도 있다.

1950년대 이후 레온티에프의 역설에 대한 많은 연구가 이루어지면서 국제무역론이 상당히 많은 발전을 이루게 되어 오늘에 이르고 있다. 그 결과 오늘날까지도 헥셔·오린모델은 국제무역의 대표적인 이론이기는 하나 산업내 무역론과 고정요소모델 또한 헥셔·오린모델을 보완하는 중요한 이론이 되었다고 할 수 있을 것이다.

지금까지 설명한 먼델·플레밍모델과 헥셔·오린모델은 국제경제학의 가장 기본적인 두 모델이다. 결국 이 두 모델의 검증방법은 국제경제학의 연구방법론이라고 해도 무방하다. 따라서 이 두 모델의 검증 방법은 미시·거시·국제경제를 종합적으로 분석해서 현실을 설명하기 위한 연구방법이 될 수 있다. 다만 헥셔·오린모델의 검증 결과는 미국에서 이미 검증된 것으로 널리 알려진 것이기 때문에 「경제이론과 현실」에서는 먼델·플레밍 모델을 검증하는데 보완하는 방법으로 활용했을 뿐이다. 특히 산업내 무역론과 레온티에프의 역설은 대기업시장 구조와 차입성장전략을 설명하는데 매우 적합하다고 할 수 있다.

5. 요약 및 결론

1. 경제모델이 통계적으로 검증이 될 수 없는 경우에는 가정과 가정으로부터 유도된 결론의 논리적 타당성(적합성) 여부를 검증할 필요성이 있다. 대표적인 것이 먼델·플레밍모델과 헥셔·오린모델이다.

2. 거시경제와 국제금융론을 통합해서 현실을 설명하기 위해서는 거시경제의 수요측면에서 통합하고 국제금융론의 측면에서 검증되어야 거시경제적 현실을 설명할 수 있고, 먼델·플레밍모델의 적합성 여부를 검증할 수 있다.

3. 거시경제의 수요측면에서 국가위험성과 예상환율과 같은 국제금융론의 주요변수를 도입해서 통합하면 먼델·플레밍모델의 적합성 여부를 검증하고 이를 평가 할 수 있는 방법이 없다. 다만 통합방법이 단순하기 때문에 정치적인 문제가 중요한 문제가 되는 경우에는 이와같은 방법을 이용할 수도 있다.

4. 정부(중앙은행)가 외환시장에 개입하지 않는 단순한 외환시장모델을 도입하면 가정상의 일관성의 문제가 해결될 수 있기 때문에 먼델·플레밍모델의 적합성 여부를 검증하고 이를 평가할 수 있다.

5. 레온티에프 역설과 그후 헥셔·오린모델의 검증결과는 먼델·플레밍모델을

검증하고 평가하는데 유용한 보완자료로 활용할 수 있다.

6. 먼델·플레밍모델과 헥셔·오린모델은 국제경제학의 기본적인 모델이기 때문에 이 두 모델의 평가방법과 그 결과는 미시·거시·국제경제를 종합적으로 분석해서 현실을 설명하는 연구방법이 될 수 있다. 「경제이론과 현실」의 연구방법은 이와같은 아이디어를 기초로 한 것이다. 이 아이디어는 필자가 1995년 부터 해외투자 프로젝트 모델을 연구하면서 얻은 것이다.

<경제 이론과 현실>연구방법론

입 증 자 료

Open-Economy Macroeconomics

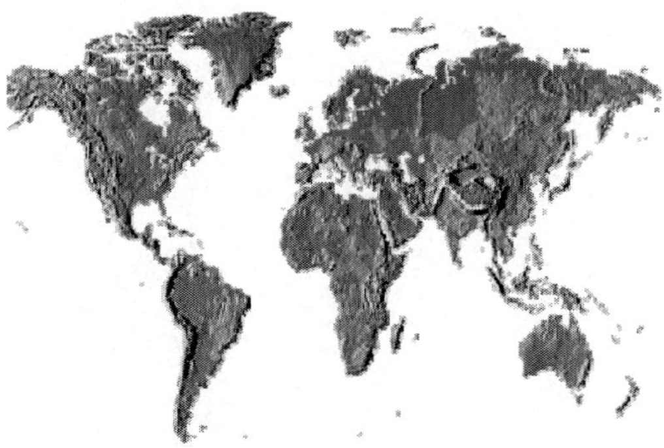

세 계 경 제 문 제 연 구 소

목 차

Ⅰ, 서 론

“거시경제와 국제금융론을 거시경제의 수요측면에서 통합하고 이를 검증한다”는 것은 경제학의 연구방법론의 기본적이고 본질적인 문제에 속한다. 이에 대한 입증자료를 정리할 필요성이 있었는데, 2006년 10월 23일 프린스턴 대학 Krugman 교수의 거시경제학 초판(2006년)에서 체계적으로 정리되어 자동적으로 입증이 되어있다는 것을 알 수 있게 되었다. 여기에 영・미 환율의 장기적인 조정과정을 더하면「경제이론과 현실」을 평가하는데 참고가 될 수 있는 것으로 생각되어 그 방법론의 입증자료로 이 팜플렛을 작성하였다.

<경제이론과 현실> 연구방법론에서 논의 된 바 있지만 거시경제의 수요측면에서 통합하는 방법은 두가지 방법이 있을 수 있다. 하나는 모델의 설정이고 또 다른 하나는 기존의 모델을 선택해서 평가하는 방법이다. 외환위기를 경제적인 현상으로 보고 이를 설명하기 위해서는 후자의 방법을 선택 할 수 밖에 없었다. 당초부터 하버드대학 Mankiw 교수의 외환위기 설명내용을 본문에서 인용하지 않고 서언에서만 언급된 것도 이와 같은 이유 때문이었다. 다만 그 내용을 여기에서 소개하는 이유는 경제학의 연구방법론의 본질적인 문제에 속하기 때문이다.

인플레이션 문제는 영국에서 제기되어 1990년대 초까지 미국에서 이론적으로 완성되었다고 할 수 있다. 이 때부터 개방경제의 장・단기 분석이 거시경제에서 본격적으로 연구되기 시작하여 오늘에 이르고 있다. 이와 같은 측면에서 볼 때도 거시경제와 국제금융론을 거시경제의 수요 측면에서 통합・검증하는 방법론은 앞으로도

중요한 연구과제가 될 것으로 생각한다.

자료를 정리하는 과정에서 우리경제의 현실에 맞도록 필요한 부분은 그 내용을 수정·보완하였고, 필요하지 않다고 생각되는 부분은 생략하였다. 그 외의 모든 것은 원래의 책의 내용과 전적으로 동일하다. 그리고 입증자료이긴 하지만 그 구성은 체계적일 필요가 있다고 생각되어 구체적으로 논의될 수 있도록 체계화하는데 최선을 다하였다.

경제학의 연구방법론은 경제학의 기본적이고 본질적인 문제이기 때문에 표절의 문제는 있을 수 없다고 생각하고 있다. 그리고 정부가 외환시장에 개입하지 않는 단순한 외환시장 모델을 도입해서 개방경제의 IS-LM 모델을 평가하는 방법도 시장경제의 기본적이고 본질적인 문제에 속한다. 끝으로 이 입증자료는 학술원에 평가자료용으로 제출하기 위해서 작성한 것이지만 앞으로 우리경제의 현실을 설명하는데 유용하게 이용할 수 있을 것으로 믿는다.

2007년 3월

정 기 옥

Ⅱ. International Interest Rate Differentials

N. Gregory Mankiw, Macroeconomics

Fifth ed., 2003, pp.327-332

정치적인 문제가 매우 중요한 문제일 경우에는 “국가위험성”으로 국가간의 이자율 격차와 외환위기를 설명할 수 있을 것이다. 그러나 외환위기를 경제적인 현상으로 보고 그 극복과정을 설명하기 위해서는 이와 같은 방법이 타당한 방법이라고 생각하지 않는다.

1. Country Risk and Exchange-Rate Expectations

So far, our analysis has assumed that the interest rate in a small open economy is equal to the world interest rate : r^*. To some extent, however, interest rates differ around the world. We now extend our analysis by considering the causes and effects of international interest - rate differentials

When we assumed earlier that the interest rate in our small open economy is determined by the world interest rate, we were applying the law of one price. We reasoned that if the domestic interest rate were above the world interest rate, people from abroad would lend to that country, driving the domestic interest rate down. And if the domestic interest rate were below the world interest rate, domestic residents would lend abroad to earn a higher return, driving the domestic interest up. In the end, the domestic interest rate would equal the world interest rate.

Why doesn't this logic always apply? There are two reasons. One reason is country risk. When investors buy U.S. government bonds or make loans to U.S. corporations, they are fairly confident that they will be repaid with interest. By contrast, in some less developed countries, it is plausible to fear that a revolution or other political upheaval might lead to a default on loan repayments. Borrowers in such conutries often have to pay higher interest rates to compensate lenders for this risk.

Another reason is expected changes in the exchange rate. Thus, because of both country risk and expectations of future exchange - rate changes, the interest rate of a small open economy can differ from interest rates in other countries around the world.

2. Differentials in the Mundell - Fleming Model

To incorporate interest - rate differentials into the Mundell - Fleming model, we assume that the interest rate in our small open economy is determined by the world interest rate plus a risk premium Θ :

$$r = r^{*} + \Theta$$

The risk premium is determined by the perceived political risk and the expected change in the real exchange rate. For our purposes here, we can take the risk premium as exogenous in order to examine how changes in risk premium affect the economy.

The model is largely the same as before. The two equations are

$$Y=C(Y-T)+I(r^*+\Theta)+G+NX(e)\ ;\ IS^*$$
$$M/p = L(r^*+\Theta,\ Y)\ ;\ LM^*$$

For any given fiscal policy, monetary policy, price level, and risk premium, this two equations determine the level of income and exchange rate that equilibriate the goods market and the money market. Holding constant the risk premium, the tools of monetary, fiscal, and trade policy work as we have already seen.

Now suppose that political turmoil causes the country's risk premium Θ to rise. The most direct effect is that the domestic interest rate rises. The higher interest rate, in turn, has two effects. First, the IS^* curve shifts to the left, because the higher interest rate reduces investment. Second, the LM^* curve shifts to the right, because the higher interest rate reduces demand for money, and this allows a higher level of income for any given money supply. Recall that Y must satisfy the equation $M/p = L(r^*+\Theta, Y)$. As figure shows, these two shifts cause income to rise and the currency to depreciate.

This analysis has an important implication : expectations of the exchange rate are partially self - fulfilling. For example, suppose that people come to believe that French franc will not be valuable in the future. Investors will place a larger risk premium on French assets : Θ will rise in France. This expectation will drive up French interest rates and, as we have just seen, will drive down the value of the French currency. Thus, the expectation that a currency will lose value in the future causes it to lose value today.

One surprising - and perhaps inaccurate - prediction of this analysis is that an increase in country risk as measured by Θ will cause the economy's income to increase. This occurs in Figure 1 because of the rightward shift in the LM^* curve. Although higher interest rates depress investment, the depreciation of the currency stimulates net exports by an even greater amount. As a result, aggregate income rises.

There are three reasons why, in practice, such a boom in income does not occur. First, the central bank might want to avoid the large depreciation of the domestic currency and, therefore, may respond by decreasing the money supply M. Second, the depreciation of the domestic currency may suddenly increase the price of imported goods, causing an increase in the price level P. Third, when some event increases the country risk premium Θ, residents of the country might respond to the same event by increasing their demand for money, because money is often the safest asset available. All three of these changes would tend to shift the LM^* curve toward the left, which mitigates the fall in the exchange

Figure 1, An increase in the Risk Premium

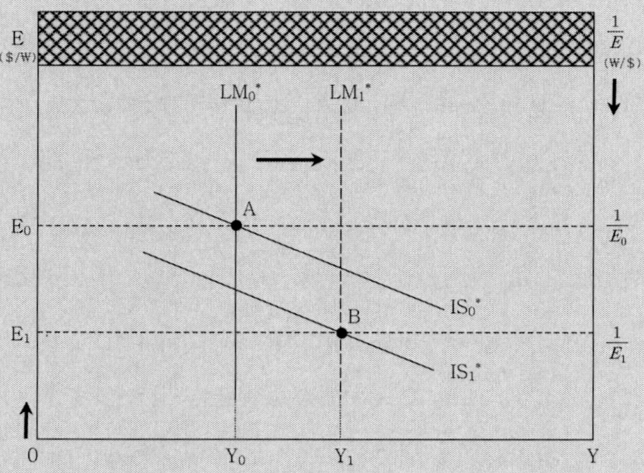

rate but also tends to depress income.

Thus, increases in country risk are not desirable.

In the short run, they typically lead to a depreciating currency and, through the three channels just described, falling aggregate income. In addition, because a higher interest rate reduces investment, the long run implication is reduced capital accumulation and lower ecomic growth.

3, International Financial Crisis : Mexico 1994-1995

In August 1994, a Mexican peso was worth 30 cents. A year later, it was worth only 16 cents. What explains this massive fall in the value of the Mexican currency? Country risk is a large part of the story.

At the beginning of 1994, Mexico was a country on the rise. The recent passage of the North American Free Trade Agreement (NAFTA), which reduced trade barriers among the United States, Canada, and Mexico, made many confident about the future of the Mexican economy. Investors around the world were eager to make loans to the Mexican government and to Mexican corporations.

Political developments soon changed that perception. A violent uprising in the Chiapas region of Mexico made the political situation in Mexico seem precarious. Then Luis Donaldo Colosio, the leading presidential candidate, was assasinated. The political future looked less certain, and many investors started placing a larger lisk premium on Mexican assets.

At first, the rising risk premium did not affect the value of the peso, because Mexico was operating with a fixed exchange rate. As we have seen, under a fixed exchange rate, the central bank agrees to trade the domestic currency (pesos) for a foreign currency (dollars) at a predetermined rate. Thus, when an increase in the country risk premium put downward pressure on the value of the peso, the Mexican central bank had to accept pesos and pay out dollars. This automatic exchange market intervention contracted the Mexican money supply (shifting LM* curve to the left) when the currency might otherwise have depreciated.

Yet Mexico's reserves of foreign currency were too small to maintain its fixed exchange rate. When Mexico ran out of dallars at the end of 1994, the Mexican government announced a devaluation of the peso. This decision had repercussion, however, because the government had repeatedly promised that it would not devalue. Investors became even more distrustful of Mexican policymakers and feared further Mexican devaluation.

Investors around the world (including those in Mexico) avoided buying Mexican assets. The country risk premium rose once again, adding to the upward pressure on interest rates and the downward pressure on the peso. The Mexican stock market plummeted. When the Mexican government needed to roll over some of its debt that was coming due, investors were unwilling to buy the new debt. Default appeared to be the government only option. In just a few months, Mexico had gone from being a promising emerging economy to being a risky economy with a government on the verge of bankruptcy.

Then the United States stepped in. The U.S. government had three motives : to help its neighbor in the south, to prevent the massive illegal immigration that might follow government default and economic collaps, and to prevent the investor pessimism regarding Mexico from spreading in other developing countries. The U.S. government, together with the International Monetary Fund (IMF), led an international effort to bail out the Mexican government. In particular, the United States provided loan guarantees for Mexican government debt, which allowed the Mexican government to refinance the debt that was coming due. The loan guarantees helped restore confidence in the Mexican economy, thereby reducing to some extent the country risk premium.

Although the U.S. loan guarantees may well have stopped a bad situation from getting worse, they did not prevent the Mexican meltdown of 1994-1995 from being a painful experience for the Mexican people. Not only did the Mexican currency lose much of its value, but Mexico also went through a deep recession. Fortunately, by the late 1990s, aggregate income was growing again, and the worst appeared to be over. But the lession from this experience is clear and could well apply again in the future : changes in perceived country risk, often attributable to political instability, are an important determinant of interest rates and exchanges rates in small open economy.

4. International Financial Crisis : Asia 1997-1998

In 1997, as the Mexican economy was recovering from its financial crisis, a similar story started to unfold in several Asian economies, including Thailand, South Korea, and especially Indonesia. The symtoms were familiar : high interest rates, falling asset value, and a depreciating currency. In Indonesia, for instance, short - term nominal interest rates rose above 50%, the stock market lost about 90% of its value, and the rupiah fell against the dollar by more than 80%. The crisis led to rising inflation in these countries because depreciating currency made imports more expensive, and to falling GDP. Real GDP in Indonesia fell about 13% in 1998, making the downturn larger than any U.S. recessions since the Great Depression of the 1930s.

The problem began in the Asian banking systems. For many years, the governments in the Asian nations had been more involved in managing the allocation of resources - in particular, financial resources - than is true in the United States and other developed countries. Some commentators had applauded this partnership between government and private enterprise and had suggested that the United States should follow the example. Over time, however, it became clear that many Asian banks had been extending loans to those with the most political clout rather than to those with the most profitable investment projects. Once rising default rates started to expose this crony capitalism as it was then called, international investors started to lose confidence in the future of these economies. The risk premium for Asian asset rose, causing interest rates to skyrocket and currencies to collaps.

International crises of confidence often involve a vicious circle that can amplify the problem. Here is one story about what happened in Asia :

1. Problems in the banking system eroded international confidence in these economies.
2. Loss of confidence raised risk premium and interest rates.
3. Rising interest rates, together with the loss of confidence, depressed the prices of stock and other assets.
4. Falling asset prices reduced the value of collateral being used for bank loans.
5. Reduced collateral increased default rates on bank loans.
6. Greater defaults exacerbated problems in the banking system. Now return to step 1 to complete and continue the circle.

Some economists have used this vicious - circle argument to suggest that the Asian crisis was a self - fulfilling propecy : bad things happened merely because people expected bad things to happen. Most economists, however, thought the political corruption of the banking system was a real problem, which was then compounded by this vicious circle of reduced confidence.

As the Asian crisis developed, the IMF and the United States tried to restore confidence, much as they had with Mexico a few years earlier. In particular, the IMF made loans to the Asian countries to help them over the crisis ; in exchange for these loans, it exacted promises that the government would reform their banking system and eliminate crony capitalism. The IMF's hope was that the short - term loans and longer - term reforms would restore confidence, lower the risk premium, and turn the vicious circle into a virtuous circle. This policy seems to have worked : the Asian economies recovered quickly from their crisis.

Ⅲ. Open - Economy Macroeconomics

P. Krugman and R. Wells. Macroeconomics,
First ed. 2006, pp. 460-485

자본의 국제적 이동(민간자본의 국제적 이동)으로 환율을 설명하기 위해서는 개방경제의 대부자금시장(금융시장)이 이에 적합하게 개선(개혁)되어야만 한다. 그렇지 않으면 환율이 거꾸로 갈 수도 있다. 이에 대해서 이 입증자료는 자세히 설명되고 있다고 생각한다.

1. Capital Flow and the Balance of Payments

A country's balance of payments accounts are a summary of the country's transactions with other countries. The most important feature of that summary is the distinction between the balance on current account and the balance on financial account.

For example, when a U.S. resident sells a good to a foreigner, that's the end of the transaction. But a financial asset, such as a bond, is different. Remember, a bond is a promise to pay interest and principal in the future. So when a U.S. resident sells a bond to a foreigner, that sale creates a liability : the U. S. resident will have to pay interest and repay principal in the future. The balance of payment accounts distinguish between transactions that don't create liabilities and those that do.

The most important feature of the U.S. balance of payments on current account was a huge deficit in the balance of payments on goods and services. How did the United States pay for all those imports? By selling a lot of assets to the rest of world, causing it to run a surplus on its financial account. A country's balance of payments on financial account, or simply financial account, is the difference between the country's sales of assets to foreigners and its purchases of assets from foreigners during a given period.

The financial account (or capital account) measures capital flows, flows of savings from one country to another. Like the current account, the financial account can be broken into several subaccounts. The most important distinction is between private and official sales and purchases - between, for example, purchases of U.S. government bonds by private investors in Europe and purchases of these bonds by the central banks of China and Japan.

The negative balance of payments on current account and the positive balance of payments on financial account for the United States in 2004 were not an accident. They reflect a basic rule of balance of payments accounting for any country :

Balance of payments on current account (CA) + Balance of payments on financial accounts (FA) = 0

or

$$CA = -FA$$

Even though the balance of payments on current account and the balance of payments on financial account sum to zero by the rules of accounting, you can see the statistical discrepancy in econonic data. Economists generally consider current account data more reliable than financial account data, so they often assume that any discrepancy represents unmeasured financial account transactions.

2. Private International Capital Flows.

We know how comparative advantage gives rise to international trade, an exchange of goods and services between countries. Our discussion of the balance of payments already tells us that the picture in international trade was somewhat simplified, because countries don't exchange just goods and services. They also trade assets - not just for other assets, but for goods and services. In fact, in 2004 inflows of capital paid for about a third of U.S. imports. That is, the United States paid for a large fraction of its imports not by exporting other goods and services but by selling assets to foreigners, creating liabilities that will have to be repaid at some future date. So it's important to understand the determinants of international capital flow.

In using the loanable funds market, we make two important simplifications :

1) We simplify the reality of international capital flows by assuming that all flows are in the form of loans. In reality, capital flows take many forms, including purchases of shares

Figure 2. The Loanable Funds Market for a Closed Economy

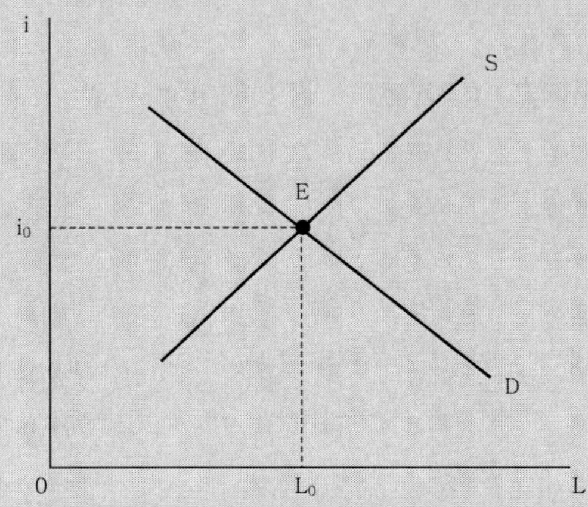

of stock in foreign companies and foreign real estate, as well as direct foreign investment, in which companies build factories or acquire other productive assets abroad.

2) We also ignore the effects of expected changes in exchange rates, the relative values of different national currencies. We will analyze the determination of exchange rates later.

Figure 2 is the loanable funds market for a closed economy. Equilibrium corresponds to point E at an interest rate of i_o, where the supply of loanable funds curve S intersects the demand for loanable funds curve D. But if international capital flows are possible, this diagram changes and E may no longer be the equilibrium. We can analize the causes and effects of international capital flows using Figure 3, which places the loanable funds market diagrams for two countries side by side.

Figure 3 illustrates a world consisting of only two countries, the United States and Korea. Panel (a) shows the loanable funds market in the U.S, where the equilibrium in the absence of international capital flows is at point E_{us} with an interest rate of i_1. Panel (b) shows the loanable funds market in Korea, where the equihbrium in the absence of international capital flows is at point E_k with an interest rate of i_2.

Will the actual interest rate in the United States remain at i_1 and in Korea at i_2 ? Not if it is easy for Korea residents to make loans to Americans. In that case, Korea lenders, attracted by high American interest rates, will lend some of their loanable funds to the United States. This capital outflow in Korea will increase the quantity of loanable funds supplied to American borrowers, pushing the U.S. interest rate down. At the same time, it will reduce the quantity of loanable funds supplied to Korea borrowers, pushing the Korea interest rate up. So, international capital flows will narrow the gap between U.S. and Korea interest rates. (In this case, Korea is assumed to be a large country).

Figure 3, International Capital Flows

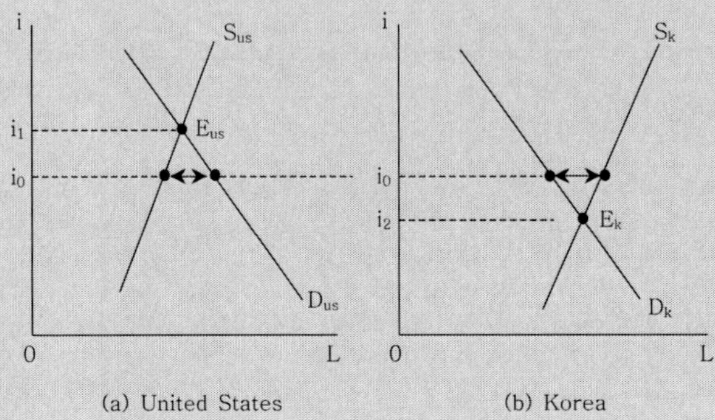

Let's further suppose that Korea lenders regard a loan to an American as being just as good as a loan to one of their compatriots, and American borrowers regard a debt to a Korea lender as no more costly than a debt to an American lender. In that case, the flow of funds from Korea to the United States will continue until the gap between their interest rates is eliminated. In other words, when residents of the two countries believe that a foreign asset is as good as a domestic one and that a foreign liability is as good as a domestic one, then international capital flows will equalize the interest rates in the two countries.

Figure 3 shows an international equilibrium in the loanable funds markets where the equilibrium interest rate is i_0 in both the United States and Korea. At this interest rate, the quantity of loanable funds demanded by American borrower exceeds the quantity of loanable funds supplied by American lenders. This gap is filled by imported funds - a capital inflow from Korea. At the same time, the quantity of loanable funds supplied by Korean lenders is greater than the quantity of loanable funds demanded by Korean borrowers. This excess is exported in the form of a capital outflow to the United States. And the two markets are in equilibrium at a common interest rate of i_0 - at that interest rate, the total quantity of loans denanded by borrowers across the two countries is equal to the total quantity of loans supplied by lenders across the two countries.

In short, international flows of capital are like international flows of goods and services. Capital moves from places where it would be cheap in the absence of international capital flows to the places where it would be expensive in the absence of such flows.

The open - economy version of the loanable funds market help us understand international capital flows in terms of the supply and demand of funds. But what underlies differences across countries in the supply and demand for funds? Why, in the absence of international capital flows, would interest rates differ internationally, creating an incentive for international capital flow?

International differences in the demand for funds reflect underlying differences in investment opportunities. In particular, a country with a rapidly growing economy, other things equal, tends to offer more investment opportunities than a country with a slowly growing economy. So rapidly growing economies typically - though not always - offer higher returns to investors than slowly growing economies in the absence of capital flows. As a result, capital tends to flow from slowly growing economies to rapidly growing economies.

International differences in the supply of funds reflect differences in savings across countries. These may be the result of differences in private savings rates, which vary widely among countries. They may be also reflect differences in savings by governments. In particular, government budget deficits, which reduce overall national saving, can lead to capital inflows.

3, Foreign Exchange Markets

We've just seen how differences in the supply of loanable funds from saving and differences in the demand for loanable funds from investment spending lead to international capital flows. We've also learned that a country's balance of payments on current account plus it's balance of payments on financial account is equal to zero : a country that generates net capital outflows must run a matching current account surplus.

The behavior of the financial account - reflecting inflows or outflows of capital - is best described by equilibrium in the international loanable funds market. At the same time, the balance of payments on goods and services, the main component of the current account, is determined by decisions in the international markets for goods and services. So given that the financial account reflects the movement of capital and the current account reflects the movement of goods and services, what ensures that the balance of payments really does balance? That is, what ensures that the two accounts actually offset one another?

The answer lies in the role of the exchange rate, which is determined in the foreign exchange market. In general, goods, services, and assets produced in a country must be paid for in that country's currency. American products must be paid for in dollars ; European products must be paid for in euros ; Japanese products must be paid for in yen. Occasionally, sellers will accept payment in foreign currency, but they will then exchange that currency for domestic money.

International transactions, then, require a market - the

foreign exchange market - in which currencies can be exchanged for each other. This market determines exchange rates, the prices at which currencies trade. In most countries people tend to express the exchange rate as the price of a dollar in domestic currency. However, there is no fixed rule. You can express the exchange rate as the price of domestic currency in terms of foreign currencies. The U.S. dollar - euro rate is commonly quoted both ways.

When discussing movements in exchange rates, economists use specialized terms to avoid confusion. When a currency becomes more valuable in terms of other currencies, economists say that the currency appreciates. When a currency becomes less valuable in terms of other currencies, it depreciates. Movements in exchage rates, other things equal, affect the relative prices of goods, services, and assets in different countries. What determines exchange rates? Supply and demand in the foreign exchange market.

1) The equilibrium exchange rate.

Figure 4 shows how the foreign exchange market works. The quantity of wons (₩) demanded and supplied at any given dollar - won exchange rate is shown on the horizontal axis, and the dollar - won exchange rate is shown on the vertical axis. The exchange rate plays the same role as the price of a good in an ordinary supply and demand diagram.

The figure shows two curves, the demand curve for wons (₩) and the supply curve for wons. The demand curve slopes downward : the more dollars it takes to buy a won, the fewer wons Americans will demand.

The key to understanding the slopes of these curves is that the level of the exchange rate affects exports and imports. When a country's currency appreciates, exports fall and imports rise. When a country's currency depreciates, exports rise and imports fall.

To understand why the demand curve for wons(₩) slopes downward, recall that the exchange rate, other things equal, determine the prices of Korean goods, services, and assets relative to those of American goods, services, and assets. If the won (₩) rises against the dollar, Korean products will become more expensive in Americans relative to American goods. So Americans will buy less from Korea and will acquire fewer wons in the foreign exchange market : the quantity of wons demanded fall as the number of dollars needed to buy a won rises. If the won falls against the dollar (the won depreciates), Korean products will become cheaper for Americans. Americans will respond by buying more from Korea and acquiring more wons in the foreign exchange market : the quantity of wons demanded rises as the number

Figure 4, The Foreign Exchange Market

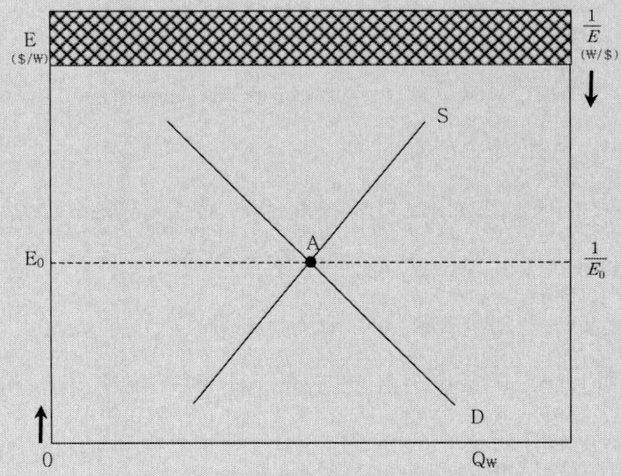

of dollars to buy a won falls.

A similar argument explains why the supply curve of wons slopes upward : the more dollars required to buy a won, the more wons Koreans will supply. Again, the reason is the effect of the exchange rate on relative prices. If the won rises against the dollar, American products look cheaper to Koreans - who will demand more of them. This will require Koreans to convert more wons into dollars.

Figure 4 is an example for the sake of simplicity. There is only two curencies in the world : dollars and wons. Americans wanting to purchase Korean goods, services, and assets come to the foreign exchange market, wanting to exchange dollars for wons. That is, Americans demand wons(₩) from the foreign exchange market and, correspondingly, supply dollars to that market. Koreans wanting to buy American goods, services, and assets come to the foreign exchange market to exchange wons for dollars. That is, Koreans supply wons to the foreign exchange market and, correspondingly, demand dollars from that market. International transfers and payments of factor income also enter into the foreign exchange market, but to make things simple we will ignore these.

The equilibrium exchange rate is the exchange rate at which the quantity of wons demanded in the foreign exchange market is equal to the quantity of wons supplied. In figure 4, the equilibrium is at point A, and the equilibrium exchange rate is E_0. At the equilibrium exchange rate, the sum of the balance of payments on current account plus the balance of payments on financial account is zero. That is, the total quantity of wons Americans want to buy is equal to the total quantity of wons Koreans want to sell.

To understand the significance of the equilibrium exchange rate, it's helpful to consider a numerical example of what equilibrium in the foreign exchange market looks like. Such an example is shown in Table 1. (This is a hypothetical table that isn't intended to match real numbers). The first row shows American purchases of wons, either to buy Korean goods, services, or to buy assets. The second row shows Korean sales of wons, either to buy American goods, services, or to buy assets.

Remember that the balance of payments accounts divide international transactions into two types. Purchases and sales of goods and services are counted in the current account. Purchases and sales of assets are counted in the financial account. At the equilibrium exchange rate, then, we have the situation shown in table 1 : the sum of the balance of payments on current account plus the balance of payments on financial account is zero.

Table 1. Equilibrium in the foreign exchange market

American purhcases of wons (trillions of wons)	To buy Korean goods and services 1.0	To buy Korean assets 1.0	Total 2.0
Korean sales of wons (trillions of wons)	To buy American goods and services 1.5	To buy American assets 0.5	Total 2.0
	Current account : -0.5	Financial account : +0.5	

2) Movements in the exchange rate.

Now lets briefly consider how a shift in the demand for wons affects equilibrium in the foreign exchange market. Suppose that for some reason, capital flows from United

States to Korea increase - say, due to a change in the preferences of American investors. The effects are shown in Figure 5. The demand for wons in the foreign exchange market increases as American investors convert dollars into wons to fund their new investments in Korea. This is shown by the shift in the demand curve from D_0 to D_1. As a result, the won appreciates : the number of dollars per won at the equilibrium exchange rate rises from E_0 to E_1

What are the consequences of this increased capital inflow for the balance of payments? The total quantity of wons supplied to the foreign exchange market still must equal the total quantity of wons demanded. So the increased capital inflow to Korea - an increase in the balance of payments on financial account - must be matched by a decline in the balance of payments on current account. What causes the balance of payments on current account to decline? The appreciations of the won. A rise in the numbers of dollars per won leads Koreans to buy more American goods and services and Americans to buy fewer Korean goods and services.

Table 2 shows how this might work. Americans are buying more Korean assets, increasing the balance on financial account from 0.5 to 1. This is offset by a reduction in American purchases of Korean goods and services and a rise in Korean purchases of American goods and services, both the

Figure 5, An Increase in the Demand for wons

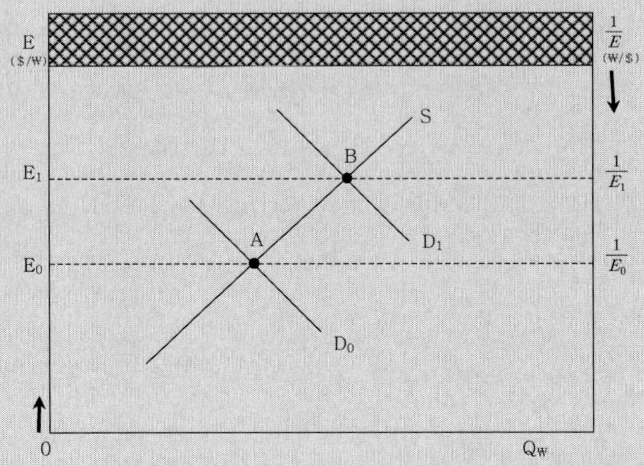

result of the won's appreciation. So any change in the balance of payments on financial account generates an equal and opposite reaction in the balance of payments on current account. Movements in the exchange rate ensure that changes in the financial account and in the current account offset each other.

Let's briefly run this process in reverse. Suppose there is a reduction in capital flows from the United States to Korea - again due to a change in the preferences of American investors. The demand for wons in the foreign exchange market falls, and the won deppreciates : the number of dollars per won at the equilibrium exchange rate falls. This leads

Koreans to buy fewer American products and Americans to buy more Korean products. So a fall in capital flows into Korea leads to a weaker won, which in turn generates an increase in net exports.

Table 2. Effects of increased capital inflows

American purncases of wons (trillions of wons)	To buy Korean goods and services 0.75	To buy Korean assets 1.5	Total 2.25
Korean sales of wons (trillions of wons)	To buy American goods and services 1.75	To buy American assets 0.5	Total 2.25
	Current account : -1.0	Financial account : +1.0	

4. Inflation and Exchange Rates

1) Inflation and real exchange rates

To take account of the effects of differences in inflation rates, economists calculate real exchange rate, exchange rates adjusted for international differences in aggregate price level. Suppose that the exchange rate we are looking at is the price of the domestic currency in terms of the foreign currency (the dollar - won rate, $/₩). Let P and P^* be indexes of the price levels in Korea and the United States, respectively.

Then the real exchange rate between the dollar and the won is defined as

$$\text{Real exchange rate(e)} = \text{dollars per won(E)} \cdot \frac{P}{P^*}$$

To distinguish it from the real exchange rate, the exchange rate unadjusted for aggregale price levels is sometimes called the nominal exchange rate.

To understand the significance of the difference between the real and nominal erchange rates, let's consider the following example. Suppose that the won appreciates 10% and Korean price index decreases from 100 to 90. At the same time, suppose that there is no change in U.S. prices, so that the U.S price index remains at 100. Then the real rate between the dollar and the won hasn't changed at all. And because the real dollar - won exchange rate dosn't changed, the nominal appreciation of the won against the U.S. dollar will have no effect, either on the quantity of goods and services exported by Korea to the United States or on the quantity of goods and services imported by Korea from the United States.

The current account responds only to changes in the real exchange rate, not the nominal exchange rate. A country's products become cheaper to foreigners only when that country's currency depreciates in real terms. As a consequence, economists who analyze movements in exports and imports of goods and services focus on the real exchange rate, not the nominal exchange rate.

2) Purchasing power parity.

A useful tool for analyzing exchange rates, closely connected to the concept of the real exchange rate, is known as purchasing power parity. The purchasing power parity between two countries currencies is the nominal exchange rate at which a given basket of goods and services would cost the same amount in each country. Suppose, for example, that a basket of goods and services that costs ＄100 in the United Stes costs 100,000 wons in Korea. Then the purchasing power parity is 1,000 wons per dollar : at that exchange rate, 100,000wons = ＄100, so the market basket costs the same amount in both countries.

Calculations of purchasing power parities are usally made by estimating the cost of buying broad market baskets containing many goods and services - everything from automobiles and groceries to housing and telephone calls. But once a year the magazine "The Economist" publishes a list of purchasing power parities based on the cost of buying a market basket that contains only one item - a McDonald's Big Mac.

Nominal exchange rates almost always differ from purchasing power parities. Some of these differences are systematic : in general, prices are lower in poor countries than in rich countries because services tend to be cheaper in poor countries. But even among countries at roughly the same level of economic development, nominal exchange rates vary quite a lot from purchasing power parity. Figure 6 shows the nomial exchange rate between the Canadian dollar and the U.S. dollar, measured as the number of canadian dollars per U.S. dollar, from 1990 to 2003, together with an estimate of the purchasing power parity exchange rate between the United States and Canada over the same period. The purchasing power parity didn't change much over the whole period because the United States and Canada had about the same rate of inflation. But at the beginning of the period the nominal exchange rate was below purchasing power parity, so a given market basket was more expensive in Canada than in the United States. By 2002 the nominal exchange rate was far above the purchasing power parity, so a market basket was much cheaper in Canada than in the United States.

Over the long run, however, purchasing power parities are pretty good at predicting actual changes in nominal exchange

Figure 6, Purchasing Power Parity versus the Nominal Exchange Rate, 1990-2003

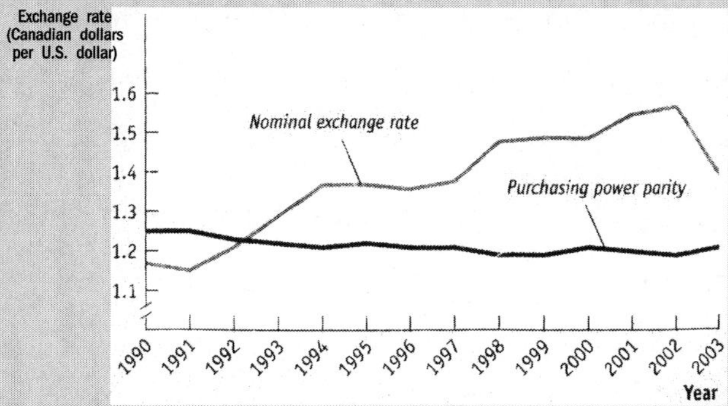

rates. In particular, nominal exchange rates between countries at similar levels of economic development tend to fluctuate around levels that lead to similar costs for a given market basket. In fact, by july 2003 the nominal exchange rate between the United States and Canada was C$ 1.22 per US $1 - just about the purchasing power parity.

5, Exchange Rate Policy

The nominal exchange rate, like other prices, is determined by supply and demand. Unlike the price of wheat or oil, however, the exchange rate is the price of a country's money in terms of another country's money. Money isn't a good or service produced by the private sector ; it's an asset whose quantity is determined by government policy. As a result, governments have much more power to influence nominal exchange rates than they have to influence ordinary prices.

The nominal exchange rate is a very important price for many countries : the exchange rate determines the price of imports ; it determines the price of exports ; in economies where exports and imports are large percentages of GDP, the movements in the exchange rate can have major effects on aggregate output and the aggregate price level. What do governments do with their power to influence this important price?

The answer is, it depends. At different times and in different places, governments have adopted a variety of exchange rate regimes. Let's talk about these regimes, how they are enforced, and how governments choose a regime. From now on we will adopt the convention that we mean the nominal exchange rate when we refer to the exchange rate.

1) Exchange rate regimes

An exchange rate regime is a rule governing policy toward the exchange rate. There are two main kinds of exchange rate regimes. A country has a fixed exchange rate when the government keep the exchange rate against some other currency at or near a particular target. A country has a floating exchange rate when the government lets the exchange rate go wherever the market takes it. This is the policy by Britain, Canada, and the United States.

Fixed exchange rates and floating exchange rates aren't the only possibilities. At various times countries have adopted compromise policies that lie somewhere between fixed and floating exchange rates. These include exchange rates that are fixed at any given time but are adjusted frequently, exchange rates that aren't fixed but are managed by the government to avoid wide swings, and exchange rates that float within a target zone but are prevented from leaving that zone. In this section, however, we will focus on the two main exchange rate regimes.

The immediate question about a fixed exchange rate is how it is possible for governments to fix the exchange rate when the exchange rate is determined by supply and demand.

2) How can an exchange rate be held fixed?

To understand how it is possible for a country to fix its exchange rate, let's consider a hypothetical country, Genovia, which for some reason has decided to fix the value of its currency, the geno, at 1.5 U.S. dollar.

The obvious problem is that \$ 1.50 may not be the equilibrium exchange rate in the foreign exchange market : The equilibrium rate may be either higher or lower than the target exchange rate.

Figure 7 shows the foreign exchange market for genos, with the quantities of genos supplied and demanded on the horizontal axis and the exchange rate of genos, measured in dollars per geno, on the vertical axis. Panel (a) shows the case in which the equilibrium value of the geno is below the target exchange rate. Panel (b) shows the case in which the equilibrium value of the geno is above the target exchange rate.

Consider the first case in which the equilibrium exchange rate is below the target exchange rate. As panel (a) of figure 7, at the target exchange rate there is a surplus of genos in the foreign exchange market, which would normally push the value of the geno down. How can the Genovian government support the value of the geno to keep the rate where it wants? There are three possible answers, all of which have been used by government at some point.

One way the Genovian government can support the geno is to soak up the surplus of genos by buying its own currency

Figure 7, Exchange Market Intervention

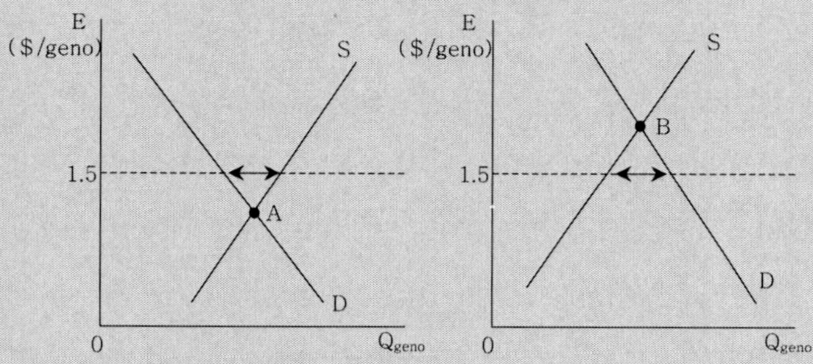

(a) Surplus at target exchange rate (b) Shortage at target exchange rate

in the foreign exchange market. Government purchase and sales of currency in the foreign exchange market are called exchange market intervention. To buy genos in the foreign exchange market, of course, the Genovian government must have U.S. dollars to exchange for genos. In fact, most countries maintain foreign exchange reserves, stocks of foreign currency, (usually U.S. dollars or euros) that they can use to buy their own currency to support its price.

We mentioned earlier that an important part of international capital flow is the result of parchases and sales of foreign assets by governments and central banks. Now we can see why gevernments sells foreign assets : they are supporting their currency through exchange market intervention.

As an alternative to exchange market intervention, the Genovian government can try shift the supply and demand curves for the geno in the foreign exchange market. Government usually do this by changing monetary policy. For example, to support the geno the Genovian central bank can raise the Genovian interest rate. This will increase capital flows into Genovia, increasing the denand for geno, at the same time that it reduces capital flows out of Genovia, reducing the supply of genos. So, other things equal, an increase in a country's interest rate will increase the value of its currency.

Finally, the Genovian government can support the geno by reducing the supply of genos to the foreign exchange market. It can do this by requiring domestic residents who want to buy foreign currency to get a license and giving these licenses only to people engaging in approved transactions (such as the purchase of imported goods the Genovian government thinks are essential). Licensing systems that limit the right of individual to buy foreign currency are called foreign exchange controls. Other things equal, foreign exchange controls increase the value of a country's currency.

So for we have been discussing a situation in which the government is trying to prevent a depreciation of the geno.

Suppose, instead, that the situation is as shown in panel (b) of figure 7, where the equilibrium value of the geno is above the target exchange rate and there is a shortage of genos. To maintain the target exchange rate, the Genovian government can apply the same three basic options in the reverse direction. It can intervene in the foreign exchange market, in this case selling genos and acquiring U.S. dollars, which it can add to its foreign exchange reserves. It can reduce the interest rates to increase the supply of genos and reduce the demand. Or it can impose foreign exchange controls that limit the ability of foreigners to buy genos. All of these actions, other things equal, will reduce the value of the geno.

As we said, all three techniques have been used to manage fixed exchange rates. But we haven't said whether fixing the exchange rate is a good idea. In fact, the choice of exchange rate regime poses a dilemma for policy markers, because fixed and floating exchange rates each have both advantages and disadvantages.

3) The exchange rate regime dilemma.

Few questions in macroeconomics produce as many argument as that of whether a country should adopt a fixed or a floating exchange rate. The reason there are so many arguments is that both sides have a case.

To understand the case for a fixed exchange rate, consider for a moment how easy it is to conduct business across state lines in the United States. There are a number of things that make interstate commerce trouble - free, but one of them is the absence of any uncertainty about the value of money : a dollar is a dollar, in both New york and Los Angeles.

By contrast, a dollar isn't a dollar in transactions between New York and Toronto. The exchange rate between the Canadian dollar and the U.S. dollar fluctuates, sometimes widely. If a U.S. firm promises to pay a Canadian firm a given number of U.S. dollars a year from now, the value of that promise in Canadian currency can vary by 10% or more. This uncertainty has the effect of detering trade between the two countries. So one benefit of a fixed exchange rate is certainty about the future value of a currency.

There is also, in some cases, an additional benefit to adopting a fixed exchange rate : by commiting itself to a fixed rate, a country is also commiting itself not to engage in inflationary policy. For exanple, in 1991 Argentina, which has a long history of irresponsible policies leading to severe inflation, adopted a fixed exchange rate of US $ 1 per Argentine peso in an attempt to commit itself to noninflationary policies in the future.

The point is that there is some economic value in having a

stable exchange rate. Indeed, as the upcoming For Inquiring Minds explains, the presumed benefits of stable exchange rates motivated the international system of fixed exchange rates created after world war II and was one major reason for creating the euro.

Unfortunately, there are also costs to fixing the exchange rate. To stabilize an exchange rate through intervention, a country must keep large quantities of foreign currency on hand - usually a low - return investment. Furthermore, even large reserves can be quickly exhausted when there are large capital flows out of a country. If a country chooses to stabilize an exchange rate by adjusting monetary policy rather than through intervention, it must divert monetary policy from other goals, notably stabilizing output and the inflation rate. Finally, exchange controls, like import quotas and tariffs, distort incentives for importing and exporting. They can also create substantial costs in terms of red tape and corruption.

So there's a delemma. Should a country let its currency float, which leaves monetary policy available for macroeconomic stabilization but creates uncertainty for business? Or should it fix the exchange rate, which eliminates the uncertainty? Different countries reach different conclusions at different times. Most European countries, except for Britain, have long believed that exchange rates among major European economies, which do most of their international trade with each other, should be fixed. But Canada seems happy with a floating exchange rate with the United States, even though the United States accounts for most of Canada's trade.

Luckily, we don't have to resolve this dilemma. For the rest of the section, we will take exchange rate regimes as given and ask how they affect macroeconomic policy.

6. Exchange Rates and Macroeconomic Policy

A look at the history of British macroeconomic policy over the past 50 years touches on all the themes we've covered in our study of macroeconomics so far : British policy makers have wrestled with inflation and unemployment and wondered how to get faster long - run growth. But British macroeconomic history also reveals other concerns - notably, whether to fix the exchange rate of the pound, and if so at what level. As we learned in the opening story, the possibility of future changes in the exchange rate regime looms large even when the exchange rate is floating. And the analysis of monetary policy focuses to a large degree on how it affects the exchange rate and the balance of payments. In other words, the fact that modern economies are open to international trade and capital flows adds a new level of complication to our analysis of macroecomomic policy. Let's look at three policy issues raised by open - economy macroeconomics.

1) Devaluation and revaluation of fixed exchange rate

Historically, fixed exchange rate haven't been permanent commitments. Sometimes countries with a fixed exchange rate switch to a floating rate, as Argentina did in 2001. In other cases they retain a fixed rate but change the target exchange rate. Such adjustments in the target were common during the Bretton wood era. A modern example is China. China maintained a fixed exchange rate against the U.S. dollar from 1994 to 2005 but changed its exchange rate regime in July 2005.

A reduction in the value of a currency that is set under a fixed exchange rate regime is called a devaluation. A devaluation is a depreciation that is due to a revision in a fixed exchange rate target. An increase in the value of a currency that is set under a fixed exchange rate regime is a called a revaluation.

A devaluation, like any depreciation, makes domestic goods cheaper in terms of foreign currency, which leads to higher exports. At the same time, it makes foreign goods more expensive in terms of domestic currency, which reduces imports. The effect is to increase the balance of payments on current account. Similarly, a revaluation makes domestic goods more expensive in terms of foreign currency, which reduces exports, and makes foreign goods cheaper in domestic currency, which increases imports. So a revaluation reduces the balance of payments on current account.

Devaluations and revaluations serve two purposes under fixed exchange rates. First, they can be used to eliminate shortages or surpluses in the foreign exchange market. For example, in early 2005, some economists were urging China to revalue the yuan so that it would not have to buy up so many U.S. dollars on the foreign exchange market.

Second, devaluations and revaluations can be used as tools of macroeconomic policy. A devaluation, by increasing exports and reducing imports, increases aggregate demand. A revaluation has the opposite effect, reducing aggregate demand.

2) Monetary policy under floating exchange rate.

Under a floating exchange rate regime, a country's central bank retains its ability to pursue independent monetary policy : it can increase aggregate demand by cutting the interest rate or decrease aggregate demand by raising the interest rate. But the exchange rate adds another dimension to the effects of monetary policy. To see why, let's return to the hypothetical of Genovia and ask what happen if the central bank cuts the interest rate.

Just as in closed economy, a lower interest rate leads to higher investment spending and higher consumption spending. But the decline in the interest rate also affects the foreign exchange market. Foreigners have less incentive to move funds into Genovia, because they will receive a lower rate of return on their loans. As a result, they have less need to exchange U.S. dollars for genos, so the demand for genos falls. At the sane time, Genovians have more incentive to move funds abroad because the rate of return on loans at home has fallen, making investments outside the country more attractive. As a result, they need to exchange more genos for U.S. dollars, so supply of genos rises.

Figure 8 shows the effect of an interest rate reduction on the foreign exchange market. The demand curve for genos shifts leftward, from D_0, to D_1, and the supply curve shifts rightward, from S_0 to S_1. The equilibrium exchange rate, as measured in U.S. dollars per geno, falls from E_0 to E_1.

The depreciation of the geno, in turn, affects aggregate demand. We have already seen how a devaluation raises exports and reduces import, thereby increasing aggregate demand. A depreciation that results from an interest rate cut

Figure 8, Monetary Policy and the Exchange Rate

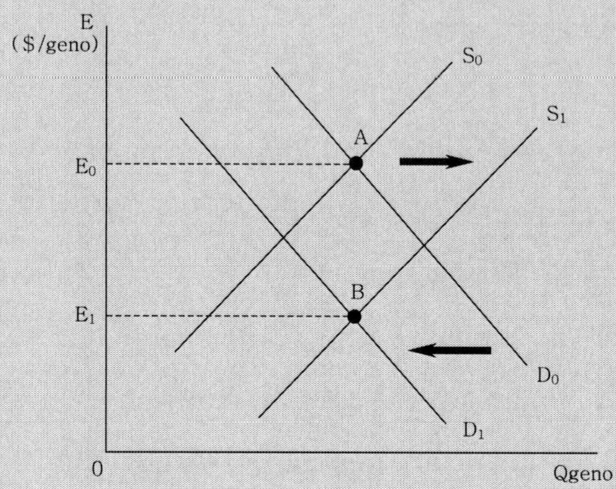

has the same effect : it increases exports and reduces imports, increasing aggregate demand.

In other words, monetary policy under floating rates has effects beyond those we have described in looking at closed economies. In a closed economy, a reduction in the interest rate leads to a rise in aggregate demand because it leads to increased investment spending and consumer spending. In an open economy with a floating exchange rate, the interest rate reduction leads to increased investment spending and consumer spending, but it also increases aggregate demand in another way : it leads to a currency depreciation, which increases exports and reduces imports, increasing aggregate demand.

3) International business cycles

Up to this point we have discussed macroeconomics, even in an open economy, as if all demand shocks originate from the domestic economy. In reality, however, economies sometimes face shocks coming from abroad. For example, recessions in the United States have historically led to recessions in Mexico.

The key point is that changes in aggregate demand affect the demand for goods and services produced abroad as well as at home : other thigs equal, a recession leads to a fall in imports and an expansion leads to a rise in imports. And one country's imports are another country's exports. This link between aggregate demand in different national economies is one reason business cycles in differene countries sometimes - but not always - seem to be synchronized. The prime example is the Great Depression, which affected countries around the world.

The extent of this link depends, however, on the exchange rate regime. To see why, think about what happens if a recession abroad reduces the demand for Genovia's exports. A reduction in foreign demand for Genovian goods and services is also a reduction in demand for genos on the foreign exchange market. If Genovia has a fixed exchange rate, it responds to this decline with exchange market intervention. But if Genovia has a floating exchange rate, the geno depreciates. Because Genovian goods and services become cheaper to foreigners when the demand for exports falls, the quantity of goods and services exported doesn't fall by as much as it would under a fixed rate. At the same time, the fall in geno makes imports more expensive to Genovians, leading to a fall in imports. Both effects limit the decline in Genovia's aggregate demand. One of the virtures of a floating exchange rate is that they help insulate countries from recessions originating abroad.

Ⅳ. Exchange Rates between the United States and the United Kingdom since 1970

Olivier Blanchard, Macroeconomics,
Fourth ed. 2006, pp.378-384

달러화에 대한 원화 환율이 안정적인 경우에도 엔화나 유로화가 약세인 경우에는 가중평균환율로 나타낸 원화가치는 상승하게 된다. 원화의 가치가 과대평가되는 중요한 요인 중에 하나가 이와 같은 이유 때문이다.

1, Nominal Exchange Rates

The real exchange rate is not directly observable, and you will not find it in the newspapers. What you will find in newspapers are nominal exchange rates, the relative prices of currencies. So, in the rest of this section, we start by looking at nominal exchange rates and then see how we can use them to construct real exchange rates.

Nominal exchange rates between two currencies can be quoted in one of two ways.

1) As the price of the domestic currency in terms of the foreign currency. If, for example, we look at the United States and the United Kingdom and think of the dollar as the domestic currency and the pound as the foreign currency, we can express the nominal exchange rate as the price of a dollar in terms of pound. In Angust 2004, the exchange rate defined this way was 0.55. In other words, 1 dollar was worth 0.55 pounds.

2) As the price of the foreign currency in terms of the domestic currency. Continuing with the same example, we can express the nominal exchange rate as the price of a pound in terms of dollars. In August 2004, the exchange rate defined

this way was 1.8. In other words, 1 pound was worth 1.8 dollars.

Either definition is fine, the important thing is to remain consistent. In this section I shall adopt the first definition. I shall define the nominal exchange rate as the price of the domestic currency in terms of foreign currency, and denote it by E. When looking at the exchange rate between the United States and the United Kingdom, E will denote the price of a dollar in terms of pounds.

Exchange rates change everyday, every minute of the day. These changes are called nominal appreciation or nominal depreciation - appreciation or depreciation for short.

You may have encountered two other words to denote movements in exchange rates : "revaluation and devaluation". These two terms are used when countries operate under fixed exchange rates - a system in which two or more countries maintain a constant exchange rate between their currencies. Under such a system, increases in the exchange rate are called revaluations rather than appreciations. Decreases in the exchange rate are called devaluations rather than depreciations.

Figure 9 plots the nominal exchange rate between the dollar and the pound since 1970. Note the two main characteristics of the figure.

Figure 9. The Nominal Exchange Rate between the Dollar and the Pound since 1970

1) The trend increase in the exchange rate. In 1970, a dollar was worth only 0.41 pounds. In 2003, a dollar was worth 0.59 pounds. Put another way, there was an appreciation of the dollar over the period.

2) The large fluctuations in the exchange rate. In the space of less than 10 years in the 1980s, the value of the dollar increased from 0.41 pounds in 1981 to 0.82 pounds in 1985, only to go back down to 0.54 pounds by early 1988. Put another way, there was a very large appreciation of the dollar in the first half of the 1980s, followed by a large depreciation later in the decade.

If we are interested, however, in the choice between domestic goods and foreign goods, the nominal exchange rate give us only part of the information we need. Figure 9, for example, tells us only about the relative price of the two currencies, the dollar and the pound.

2. Real Exchange Rates

How can we construct the real exchange rate between the United States and the United Kingdom - the price of U.S. goods in terms of British goods ?

Suppose the United States produced only one good, a Cadillac Seville Luxury Sedan, and the United Kingdom also produced only one good - a Jaguar. The price of the U.S. goods (Cadillacs) in terms of British goods (Jaguars) would be straightforward. We would express both goods in terms of same currency and then compute their relative price.

Suppose, for example, we expressed both goods in terms of pounds. Then :

The first step would be to take the price of a Cadillac in dollars and convert it to a price in pounds. The price of a Cadillac in the United States is $40,000. A dollar is worth 0.55 pounds, so the price of a Cadillac in pounds is $40,000×0.55= £22,000

The second step would be to compute the ratio of the price of the Cadillac in pounds to the price of the Jaguar in pounds. The price of a Jaguar in the United Kingdom is £ 30,000, So the price of a cadillac in terms of Jaguars - that is, the real exchange rate - would be 22,000 / 30,000 = 0.73.

The example is straightforward, but how do we generalize it ? The United States and the United Kingdom produce more than Cadillacs and Jaguars, and we want to construct a real exchange rate that reflects the relative price of all the goods produced in the United States in terms of all the goods produced in the United Kingdom.

The computation we just went through tells us how to proceed. Rather than using the price of a Jaguar and the price of a Cadillac, we must use a price index for all goods produced in the United Kingdom and a price index for all goods produced in the United States. Let P be the GDP deflator for the United States, P^* be the GDP deflator for the United Kingdom, and E be the dollar - pound nominal exchange rate. The real exchange rate is given by

$$e = \frac{EP}{P^*}$$

The price of U.S goods in dollars is P. Multiplying it by the exchange rate, E - the price of dollars in terms of pounds - gives us the price of U.S. goods in pounds, EP.

The price of British goods in pounds is P.* Thus, the real exchange rate (the price of U.S. goods in terms of British goods) is $e = \frac{EP}{P^*}$. That is, the real exchange rate is constructed by multiplying the domestic price level by the nominal exchange rate and then dividing by the foreign price level - a straightforward extension of the computation we made in our Cadillac/Jaguar example.

Unlike the price of Cadillacs in terms of Jaguars, the real exchange rate is an index number. That is, its level is arbitray and, therefore, uninformative. It is uninformative, because the GDP deflators used to construct the real exchange rate are index number. They are equal to one (or 100) in whatever year is chosen as the base year.

But all is not lost. Although the level of real exchange rate is uninformative, the rate of change of the real exchange rate is informative. If, for example, the real exchange rate between the United States and the United Kingdom increases by 10%, this 10% increase tells us that U.S. goods are now 10% more expensive relative to British goods than they were before.

Like nominal exchange rates, real exchange rates move over time. This changes are called real appreciations or real depreciations. An increase in the real exchange rate, that is, an increase in the relative price of domestic goods in terms of foreign goods, is called a real appreciation. A decrease in the real exchange rate, that is, a decrease in the relative price of domestic goods in terms of foreign goods. is called a real depreciation.

Figure 10 plots the evolution of the real exchange rate between the United States and the United Kingdom from 1970 to 2003. For convenience, it also reproduces the evolution of the nominal exchange rate from Figure 9. The GDP deflators have both been set equal to one in the first quarter of 2000, so the nominal exchange rate and the real exchange rate are equal in that quarter by construction.

Note the two main characteristics of Figure 10. While the nominal exchange rate went up during the period, the real exchange rate went down. In 1970, the real exchange rate was equal to 1.7, it was down to 1.0 in 2003.

How do we reconcile the fact that there was both a nominal appreciation and a real depreciation during the period? To see why, return to the definition of the real exchange rate :

$$e = E \cdot \frac{P}{P^*}$$

Two things have happened since 1970.

Figure 10, Real and Nominal Exchange Rates between the United States and the United Kingdom since 1970

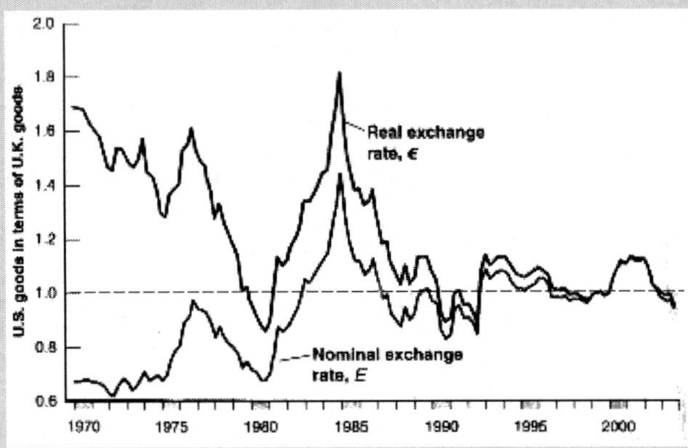

1) First, E has increased. The dollar has gone up in terms of pounds. This is the nominal appreciation.

2) Second, P/P^* has decreased. The price level has increased less in the United States than in the United Kingdom. Put another way, over the period, average inflation has been lower in the United States than in the United Kingdom.

The resulting decrease in P/P^* has been larger than the increase in E, leading to a decrease in e, a real depreciation - a decrease in the relative price of domestic goods in terms of foreign goods.

There is a general lesson here. Over long periods of time, differences in inflation rates across countries can lead to very different movements in nominal exchange rates and real exchange rates.

This is not surprising. Year - to - year movements in the price ratio, P/P^*, are typically small compared to the often sharp movement in the nominal exchange rate, E. Thus, from year to year, or even over the course of a few years, movements in the real exchange rate, e, tend to be driven mostly by movements in the nominal exchange rate, E. Note that since the early 1990s, the nominal exchange rate and the real exchange rate have moved nearly together. This reflects the fact that, since the mid - 1980s, inflation rates have been very similar in both countries.

3, Multilateral Exchange Rates

We have so far concentrated on the exchange rate between the United States and the United Kingdom. But the United Kingdom is just one of many countries the United States trades with. How do we go from bilateral exchange rates to multilateral exchange rates that reflect the geographic composition of U.S. trade for both exports and imports?

The answer is straightforward. If we want to measure the

average price of U.S. goods relative to the average price of goods of the trading partners of the United States, we should use the U.S. share of trade with each country as the weight for that country. Using export shares, we can construct an "export" real exchange rate, and using import shares, we can construct an "import" real exchange rate. Because economists usually do not want to keep track of two different exchange rates, they typically use an exchange rate that takes an average of export and import shares. This is the variable we will think of when we talk about the multilateral real U.S. exchange rate, or the U.S. real exchange rate for short.

Figure 11 shows the evolution of this multilateral real exchange rate, the price of U.S. goods in terms of foreign goods, from 1973 to 2003. Like the bilateral real exchange rates, it is an index number. So its level is also arbitrary ; here it is set equal to one in the first quater of 2000.

The most striking aspect of the figure is the large swing in the real exchange rate in the 1980s. U.S. goods were about 40% more expensive relative to foreign goods in the mid - 1980s than they were either at the begining or at the end of the decade. In other words, there was a large real appreciation in the first half of the 1980s, followed by an even larger real depreciation in the second half.

This large swing, which has its origins in the movement of

Figure 11, The U.S. Multilateral Real Exchange Rate since 1973

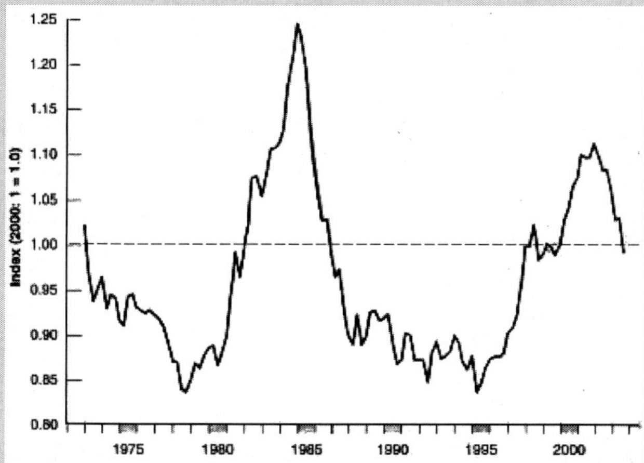

the nominal exchange rate, is so striking that it has been given various names, from the "dollar cycle" to the more graphic "dance of the dollar." Note the similar but smaller movements of the dollar from the mid - 1990s on, including an increase of 25% from 1995 to 2001, and a decrease since then. Many economists wonder whether we are in the middle of a second large swing, a second dollar cycle.

V. 결 론

「경제이론과 현실」의 종결편 "경제학의 조류"는 제1권 미시경제와 제2권 거시경제를 검증하는 내용으로 구성된 것이었고, 원래 1995년 부터 해외투자 프로젝트모델을 연구하면서 얻게된 아이디어를 기초로한 것이었다. 이에 대해서 입증된 결과를 방법론의 측면에서 요약하면 다음과 같다.

1) 단순한 외환시장 모델을 도입하면 거시경제의 수요측면에서 거시경제와 국제금융론이 이론적으로 통합이 가능하다.

2) 자본의 국제적 이동이 외국인의 직·간접 투자로 인한 자본의 유입에 의해서 일방적으로 이루어지는 경우에는 원화의 가치가 과대평가 될 수 있기 때문에 구매력평가설에 의한 적정환율을 장기환율로 보고 현실을 설명할 수 있다. 다만 실제적인 환율은 적정환율보다 높을 수도 있고 낮을 수도 있기 때문에 2006년 3월의 환율을 "적정환율 범위"내의 환율이라고 가정했을 뿐이다.(Epilogue 참조)

3) 외환보유고를 적정수준까지 늘리고 외환위기를 단기간에 성공적으로 극복하기 위해서는 중앙은행의 외환시장 개입은 필연적인 것이라고 할 수 있다.

4) 외환위기는 경제성장이나 발전론적인 측면에서 분석하는 것이 타당하다.(Appendix 1 참조)

5) 개방경제의 IS-LM모델(Mundell-Fleming Model)은 세계적인 일반론일 뿐만 아니라 이 이론을 받아들여야 우리경제의 거시경제적 현실을 설명할 수 있다.

6) 변동환율제도에서도 환율을 안정시킬 필요성이 있을 때는 고정환율제도에서 이용되는 각종 환율정책을 도입할 수 있다.

7) 이자율이 하락할 때 환율(원·달러 환율)이 상승하고 순수출

이 증가되기 위해서는 주식시장과 부동산 시장 및 외환시장을 통합 조정할 필요성이 있다.(Appendix 2 참조)

8) 원화의 가치가 과대평가되어 원·달러환율이 매우 낮은 수준에 있을 경우에는 외국인의 자본이 유출되고, 한국인의 해외투자도 증가할 것이기 때문에 앞으로 외환시장을 선진화 하는 것은 매우 중요한 정책목표가 될 수밖에 없을 것으로 생각한다.

이상의 요약은 개방경제의 IS-LM모델(Mundell-Fleming Model)을 국제금융론의 측면에서 검증하고 입증한 결과를 토대로 한 것이다. 따라서 국가위험성이나 예상환율과 같은 국제금융론상의 중요변수를 도입해서 거시경제와 국제금융론을 통합하고 외환위기를 설명하는 것은 옳은 방법이라고 할 수 없다. 다만 정치적인 변수가 매우 중요한 변수일 경우에는 이와 같은 방법에 의존할 수도 있다.

실업과 인플레이션의 문제가 필립스곡선(Phillips curve)에 의해서 설명되는 것에서도 알 수 있는 바와 같이 인플레이션의 문제는 1958년 영국에서 제기 되어 1990년대 초반에 이르러서야 미국에서 이론적으로 완성되었다.(Appendix 4 참조) 개방경제의 장·단기 분석이 거시이론에서 체계화 되기 시작한 것이 이때부터이며, 우리경제의 외환위기 본질적인 요인도 인플레이션에 의해서 환율이 장기적으로 조정되지 않았기 때문이었다. 따라서 영·미 환율의 장기적인 조정과정은「경제이론과 현실」을 평가하는데 참고가 될 수 있을 뿐만아니라 우리경제의 원·달러환율의 변동과정을 설명하는데에도 유용하게 이용될 수 있을 것으로 생각한다.

다행히 <경제이론과 현실> 연구방법론을 입증까지 할 수 있는 기회가 되어 심사용으로 이 자료를 작성하였다. 그 동안 학술원 임직원 여러분께 여러가지로 심려를 끼쳐드려 송구스럽게 생각하며 이로서 입증에 대신하고자 한다.

도서 주요내용 및 학문적 기여도

<제1권, 미시경제>

1999년 먼델(Mundell)이 국제금융론에 대한 이론적인 공로로 노벨경제학상을 수상하고, 2000년 하버드대학의 맨큐(Mankiw)교수가 이를 근거로 우리경제를 포함한 후진국의 외환위기를 설명하였다. 그러나 이는 개방경제의 거시이론의 수요측면만을 분석의 대상으로 하고 있는 것이다. 따라서 이에 대한 공급측면이 분석 되어야만 우리경제의 현실을 설명할 수 있게 된다.

1970년대말 이후 우리경제의 산업화 과정에서 중요한 문제로 끊임없이 제기되어온 문제가 대기업의 시장구조문제와 차입성장전략(경상수지적자)의 문제였다. 이 문제는 앞으로 우리경제가 채권국으로서의 선진국으로 성장하는 경우에도 그 이론적 근거는 똑같고, 대기업도 중요한 역할을 할 것으로 보이기 때문에 중요한 연구과제가 될 수밖에 없을 것으로 보인다. 따라서 이와 같은 현실적인 문제를 설명할 수 있는 경제이론 또는 경제모델을 어떻게 선택할 것인가하는 문제가 미시경제의 주요연구과제가 될 수밖에 없을 것이다.

대기업과 차입성장전략의 문제를 설명할 수 있는 모델이 미시경제이론에서 체계적으로 분석되어야만 개방경제의 거시이론의 공급측면을 설명할 수 있다. 이와같은 점을 감안해서 게임이론과 시장구조론, 저축과 투자 및 이자율 결정이론, 기업의 투자결정이론등을 개방경제의 거시이론의 공급측면의 분석에 적합하도록 경제모델을 선택하고 이를 체계적으로 구성하였다. 그 외에도 외환 위기극복 과정에서 중요한 문제로 부각되고 있는 공평성의 문제도 쉽게 접근할 수 있도록 하였다.

이 책은 외환위기라는 특수한 상황에서 개방경제의 거시이론의 공급측면의 이론적 근거를 체계화 하기 위해서 쓰여진 것이지만 앞으로도 개방경제의 거시이론의 공급측면의 이론적 발전에 기여할 수 있는 것으로 생각한다.

<제2권, 거시경제>

외환위기는 본질적으로 거시경제 문제가 아니라 국제금융의 문제이다. 그러나 국제금융론은 「개방경제의 거시이론」이라고 하는 바와 같이 개방경제의 총수요를 분석하는 것을 주요목적으로 하고 있다. 따라서 외환위기시에는 거시경제의 수요측면에서 거시경제와 국제금융론을 통합해야만 현실을 설명할 수 있게 된다.

거시경제의 수요측면에서 통합하는 방법은 수식으로 통합하는 방법과 이론적으로 통합하는 방법이 있을 수 있다. 수식으로 통합하는 방법은 국가위험성과 예상환율과 같은 국제금융론상의 주요변수를 도입해서 통합하는 방법이다. 따라서 이는 통합방법이 매우 단순하기는 하지만 국제금융론의 측면에서 먼델·플레밍 모델을 검증할 수 있는 방법이 없다는데 문제가 있다.

위와같은 이유 때문에 현실을 설명하기 위해서는 정부(중앙은행)가 외환시장에 개입하지 않는 단순한 외환시장모델을 이용해서 거시경제와 국제금융론이 이론적으로 통합되어야 한다. 이와같은 방법에 의하면 개방경제의 거시이론의 수요측면을 검증할 수 있기 때문이다.

개방경제의 거시이론의 공급측면에서 볼때 외환위기는 외채위기의 측면에서 분석되어야 한다. 따라서 대기업과 차입성장전략으로 인한 외채위기는 산업화 과정으로서의 경제발전이나 경제성장의 측면에서 분석하고 있다. 이를 설명할 수 있는 이론이 고정요소모델과 이시점간 국제무역론 및 산업내 무역론이다. 이는 레온티에프의 역설과 그 이후 헥셔 오린모델의 검증결과를 참고한 것이었다.

<제3권, 종결편, 경제학의 조류>

먼델·플레밍모델을 통계적으로 검증할 수 없다고 해서 이를 부정할 수는 없기 때문에, 우리경제의 입장에서 이를 이론적으로 검증 평가해서 어떻게 보완할 것인가하는 문제가 무엇보다도 중요한 과제일 수 밖에 없다. 왜냐하면 먼델·플레밍 모델은 세계적인 일반이론일뿐만 아니라 이 모델을 받아들여야지만 거시경제적 현실을 설명할 수 있기 때문이다.

경제모델을 통계적으로 검증할 수 없는 경우에는 모델의 가정과 가정으로부터 유도된 결론의 논리적 타당성 여부를 검증해야 한다. 정부(중앙은행)가 외환시장에 개입하지 않는 단순한 외환시장모델을 도입하면 먼델·플레밍 모델의 검증평가가 가능하다.

외국에서 개발되고 외국에서 검증된 경제모델을 우리경제의 입장에서 검증하는 것은 「경제이론과 현실」의 연구방법론일 수 밖에 없다. 왜냐하면 기존의 외국의 책과는 다른 책이 될 수 밖에 없기 때문이다. 특히 이 책은 세계경제적인 측면에서 검증되고 있기 때문에 다른 국가의 경제현실을 설명하는 연구방법으로도 활용할 수 있을 것으로 생각한다.

먼델·플레밍모델의 검증방법은 레온티에프의 역설과 그 후 헥셔·오린모델의 검증방법을 참고하였다. 이 두 모델의 검증방법은 미시·거시·국제경제이론을 종합적으로 분석하여 현실을 설명하는데 유용한 연구방법론이 될 수 있다.

Epilogue

Empirical Tests of the Purchasing - Power Parity Theory

D. Salvatore, International Economics
Seventh ed. 2001, PP. 508-514

환율은 자국화폐의 가치로 설명할 수도 있고 외국화폐의 가치로 설명할 수도 있다. 지금까지는 자국화폐의 가치로 설명되고 있으나 이 입증자료는 외국화폐의 가치로 설명되고 있다. 일관성이 없다고 할 수 있지만 입증자료이기 때문이다.

1, Absolute Purchasing - Power Parity Theory

In this section, we examine the purchasing-power parity(PPP) theory and evaluate its usefulness in explaining exchange rates. The purchasing-power parity(PPP) theory was elaborated and brought back into use by the Swedish economist Gustav Cassel in order to estimate the equilibrium exchange rate at which nations could return to the gold standard after the disruption of international trade and the large changes in relative commodity prices in the various nations caused by World War I. There is an absolute and a relative version of the PPP theory. These will be examined in turn.

The absolute purchasing - power parity theory postulates that the equilibrium exchange rate between two currencies is equal to the ratio of the price levels in the two nations. Specifically :

$$E = \frac{P}{P^*}$$

Where E is the exchange rate or spot rate and P and P^* are, respectively, the general price level in the home nation and in the foreign nation. For example, if the price of one bushel of wheat is $2 in the United States and £1 in the United Kingdom, then the exchange rate between the dollar and the pound should be E=$2/£1 = 2. That is, according to the law of one price, a given commodity should have the same price in both countries when expressed in terms of the same currency. If the price of one bushel of wheat in terms of dollar were $1 in the United States and $3 in the United Kingdom, firms would purchase wheat in the United States and resell it in Britain at a profit. This commodity arbitrage would cause the price of wheat to fall in Britain and rise in the United States until the prices were equal, say $2 per bashel, in both countries. Commodity arbitrage thus operates just as does currency arbitrage in equalizing commodity prices throught the market.

This version of the PPP theory can be very misleading. There are several reasons for this. First, it appears to give the exchange rate that equilibriate trade in goods and services while completely disregarding the capital account. Thus, a nation experiencing capital outflows would have a deficit in its balance of payment, while a nation receiving capital inflows would have a surplus. Second, this version of the PPP theory will not even give the exchange rate that equilibrates trade in goods and services because of the existence of many nontraded goods and services.

Nontraded goods include products, such as cement and bricks, for which the cost of transportation is too high for them to enter international trade. Most services also do not enter international trade. International trade tends to equalize the prices of traded goods and services among nations but not the prices of nontraded goods and services. Since the general price level in each nation includes both traded and nontraded commodities, and prices of the latter are not equalized by international trade, the absolute PPP theory will not lead to the exchange rate that equilibrated trade. Furthermore, the absolute PPP theory fails to take into account transportation costs or other obstruction to the free flow of international trade. As a result, the absolute PPP theory cannot be taken too seriously. Whenever the purchasing-power parity theory is used, it is usually in its relative formulation.

2, Relative Purchasing-Power Parity Theory.

The more refined relative purchasing-power parity theory postulates that the change in the exchange rate over a period of time should be proportional to the relative change in the price levels in the two nations over the same time period. Specifically, if we let the subscript o refer to the base period and 1 to a subsequent period, the relative PPP theory postulates that

$$E_1 = \left(\frac{P_1}{P_0} \ / \ \frac{P_1^*}{P_0^*} \right) \cdot E_0$$

Where E_1 and E_0 are, respectively, the exchange rates in period 1 and in the base period.

For example, if the general price revel does not change in the foreign nation from the base period to period 1, while the general price level in the home nation increases by 50 percent, the relative PPP theory postulates that the exchange rate should be 50% higher in period 1 as compared with the base period.

Note that if the absolute PPP held, the relative PPP would also hold, but when the relative PPP holds, the absolute PPP need not hold. For example, while the very existence of capital flows, transportation costs, other obstructions to the free flow of international trade, and government intervention policies leads to the rejection of the absolute PPP, only a change in these would lead the relative PPP theory astray.

However, other difficulties remain with the relative PPP theory. One of these results from the fact that the ratio of the price of nontraded to the price of traded goods and services is systematically higher in developed nations than in developing nations. One reason that they give for this is that techniques in the production of many nontraded goods and services are often quite similar in developed and developing countries. However, for labor to remain in these occupations in developed nations, it must receive wages comparable to the high wages in the production of traded goods and services. This makes the price of nontraded goods and services systematically much higher in developed nations than in developing nations. For example, the price of a haircut may be $10 in the United States but only $1 in Brazil.

Since the general price index includes the prices of both traded and nontraded goods and services, and prices of the latter are not equalized by international trade, but are relatively higher in developed nations, the relative PPP theory will tend to predict overvalued exchange rates for developed nations and undervalued exchanges rates for developing nations, with distortion being greater the greater the differences in the levels of development.

Significant structural changes also lead to problems with the relative PPP theory. For example, the PPP theory indicated that the British pound was undervalued immediately after World War 1. The reason was that the United Kingdom had liquidated many of its foreign investments during the war, so that the equilibrium exchange rate predicted by the relative PPP theory would have left a large deficit in the U.K. balance of payments after the war.

3, A Simple Test of Relative Purchasing - Power Parity Theory

Table 3 presents data that can be used as a test of the relative purchasing-power parity theory over the period 1973-1999. The first column give the inflation rate in each of the major six industrial countries minus the U.S. inflation rate. The second column gives the rate of depreciation of the national currency relative to the U.S. dollar over the same period. This inflation rate is measured by the percentage change in the GDP deflator. Note that a negative value in the first column means that the nation faced smaller rate of inflation than the United States, while a negative value in the second column means that the nation's currency appreciated with respect to U.S. dollar.

Table 3. Differences in Relative Inflation rates and Currency Depreciation, 1973-1999

Country	Inflation Difference	Currency Depreciation
Japan	-33.2	-78.5
Germany	-29.8	-38.2
France	20.4	31.1
United Kingdom	44.6	41.0
Italy	63.0	101.4
Canada	4.8	33.8

If the relative version of the PPP theory held exactly, the values for the national inflation rates minus the U.S. inflation rate would be identical to the percentage depreciation of the national currency relative to the U.S. dollar for each country. Since the actual values exhibit large differences, however, the relative PPP theory did not seem to work very well. This is only a crude test ; more refined and general tests are discussed in the following section.

4, Empirical Tests of the Purchasing - Power Parity Theory

The movement to a floating exchange rate system since 1973 stimulated a great resurgence of interest in the purchasing - power parity theory and led to numerous empirical studies to test the validity of the theory

Frenkel(1978) provided empirical evidence on the long-run validity of the PPP theory during the high inflation years of the 1920s, and so did Kravis and Lipsey(1978) for the 1950-1970 period and McKinnon(1979) for the 1953-1977 period. On the other hand, Frenkel(1981) found that the PPP theory collapsed during the 1970s, especially in the latter part of the 1970s, and so did Levich(1985) and Dornbush(1987) for the 1980s.

Frankel(1986, 1990) has suggested that researchers must utilize data over many decades to properly test the PPP theory because deviations from purchasing-power parity die out only very slowly. Utilizing annual data on the dollar - pound exchange rate over the 1869-1984 period, Frankel showed that it took between four and five years for one-half of the deviation from PPP to die out and that only about 15% of the deviation from PPP were eliminated per year. Lothian and Taylor(1996), using data from 1790 to 1990 for the dollar / pound and the franc / pound exchange rates, confirmed Frankel's results, as did Frankel and Rose(1995) using annual data for 150 countries from 1948 to 1992, and many other recent empirical studies.

Why do deviations from PPP die out so slowly? One possible explanation given by Rogoff(1996 and 1999) is that, despite all the globalization that has occurred during the past two or three decades, international commodity markets are still much less integrated than national commodity markets. This is due to the existence of transportation costs, trade protection, information costs, and very limited international labor mobility.

We can thus come to following overall conclusion with regard to the empirical relevance of the PPP theory. (1) We expect the PPP theory to work well for highly traded individual commodities, but less well for all traded goods together, and not so well for all goods (which include many nontraded commodities). (2) For any level of aggregation, the PPP theory works reasonably well over very long periods of time(many decades), but not so well over one or two decades, and not well at all in the short run. (3) PPP works well in case of purely monetary disturbances and in inflationary periods, but not so well in periods of monetary stability, and not well at all in situations of major structural changes.

These conclusions are very important not only for the relevance of PPP theory itself, but also because the PPP theory occupies a central position in the monetary and in the asset market or portfolio balance approaches to the balance-of-payments and exchange rate determination.

Appendix 1

Convergence Hypothesis

P. Krugman and R. Wells. Macroeconomics,
First ed. 2006, PP. 202-206

세계의 소득수준의 균등화 가설(convergence hypothesis)만 가지고는 우리 경제의 성공을 설명하는데 부족하다. 왜냐하면 경제성장의 수출 의존도가 매우 높기 때문이다. 이것이 성공할 수 있었던 중요한 요인 중에 하나는 이미 설명한 바와 같이 그동안 국제무역론이 우리 경제의 대기업 시장 구조와 차입성장 전략에 매우 유리하게 발전해 왔기 때문이라고 할 수 있다.

1, Success, Disappointment, and Failure

As we've seen, rates of long-run economic growth differ quite a lot around the world. We conclude this chapter with a look at three regions of the world that have had quite different experiences with economic growth over the last few decades.

Figure 12 shows trends since 1960 in real GDP per capita for three countries : Argentina, Ghana, and South Korea. We have chosen these countries because each is a particular striking example of what has happened in its region.

South Korea's amazing rise is part of a broad "economic miracle" in East Asia. Argentina's stagnant real GDP per capita is more or less typical of the disappointment that has characterized latin America. And Ghana unhappy story is, unfortunately, typical of Africa experience.

Figure 12, Success, Disappointment, and Failure

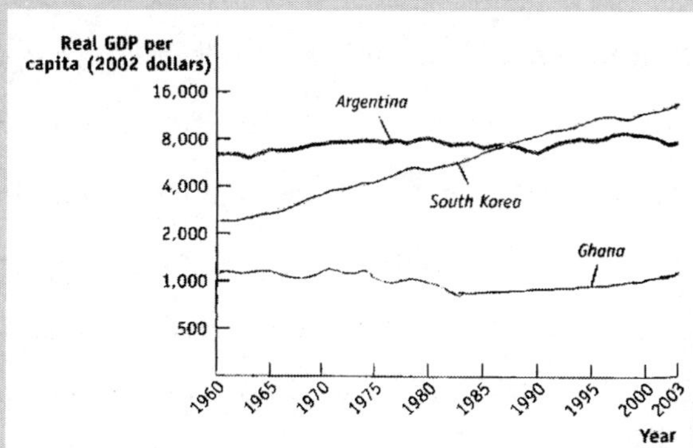

2, The East Asian Miracle

In 1960 South Korea was a very poor country. In fact, in 1960 its real GDP per capita was lower than that of India today. But as you can see from Figure 12, beginning in the early 1960s South Korea began an extremely rapid economic ascent : real GDP per capita grew about 7% per year for more than 30 years. Today South Korea, though still some what poorer than Europe or the United States, looks very much like an economically advanced country.

South Korea's ecomic growth is unprecedented in history : it took the country only 35 years to achieve growth that required centries elsewhere. Yet South Korea is only part of a broader phenomenon, often referred to as the East Asia economic miracle. High growth rates first appeared in South Korea, Taiwan, Hong Kong, and Singapore but then spread across the region, most notably to China. Since 1975 the whole region has increased real GDP per capita by 6% per year, three times America's historical rate of growth.

How have the Asian countries achieved such high growth rates? The answer is that all of the sources of productivity growth have been firing on all cylinders. Very high saving rates, the percentage of GDP that is saved nationally in any given year, have allowed the countries to significantly increase the amount of physical capital per worker. Very good basic education has permitted a rapid improvement in human capital. And these countries have experienced substantial technological progress.

Why hasn't any economy achieved this kind of growth in the past? Most economic analysts think that East Asia's growth spurt was possible because of its relative backwardness. That is, by the time that East Asian economies began to move into the modern world, they could benefit from adopting the technological advances that had been generated in technological advanced countries such as the United States. In 1900, the United States could not have moved quickly to a modern level of productivity because much of technology that powers the modern economy, from jet plance to computers, hasn't been invented yet. In 1970, South Korea probably still had lower labor productivity than the United States had in 1900, but it could rapidly upgrade its productivity by adopting technology that had been developed in the United States, Europe, and Japan over the previous century.

The East Asian experience demonstrates that economic growth can be especially fast in countries that are playing catch-up to other countries with higher GDP per capita. On this basis many economists have suggested a general principle known as the convergence hypothesis. It says that differences in real GDP per capita among countries tend to narrow over time because countries that start with lower real GDP per capita tend to have higher growth rates.

We will look at the evidence on convergence hypothesis. Even before we get to that evidence, however, we can say right away that starting with a relatively low level of real GDP per capita is no guarantee of rapid growth, as the examples of Latin America and Africa both demonstrate.

3, Latin America's Disappointment

In 1900, Latin America was not regarded as an economically backward region. Natural resources, including both cultivatable land and minerals, were abundant. Some countries, notably Argentina, attracted millions of immigrants from Europe. Measures of real GDP per capita in Argentina, Uruguay, and southern Brazil were comparable to that in economically advanced countries

Since about 1920, however, growth in Latin America has been disappointing. As Figure 12 shows in the case of Argentina, it has remained disappointing to this day. The fact that South Korea is now much richer than Argentina would have seemed inconceivable a few generation ago.

Why has Latin America stagnated? Comparisons with East Asian success stories suggest several factors. The rates of saving and investment spending in Latin America have been much lower than in East Asia, partly as a result of irresponsible government policy that has eroded saving through high inflation, bank failures, and other disruptions.

Education – especially broad basic education – has been underemphasized : even Latin America rich in natural resources often failed to channel that wealth into their educational systems. And political instability, leading to irresponsible economic policies, has taken a toll.

In the 1980s, many economists came to believe that Latin America was suffering from excessive government intervention in market. They recommended opening the economies to imports, selling off government-owned companies and, in general, freeing up individual initiative. The hope was that this would produce an East Asian type economic surge. So Far, however, only one Latin American nation, Chile, has achieved really rapid growth. It now seems that pulling off an economic miracle is a harder than it looks

4, Africa's Troubles.

Africa south of the Sahara is home to about 600 million

people, more than twice the population of the United States. On average they are very poor, nowhere close to U.S. living standard 100 or even 200 years ago. Worst of all, Africa's economies have been moving backward : average real GDP per capita in 2003 was 11% lower than in 1974.

The consequence of this poor growth performance has been intense and worsening poverty. In 1970, 42% of Africans lived on less than $ 1 a day in today's prices. By 2001, that number was 46%

This is very disheartening picture. What explains it ? Several factors are probably crucial. Perhaps first and foremost is the problem of political instability. In the years since 1975, large parts of Africa have experienced savage civil wars that have killed millions of people and made productive investment spending impossible. The threat of war and general anarchy has also inhibited other important preconditions for growth, such us education and provision of necessary infrastructure.

Property rights are also a problem. The lack of legal safeguards means that property owners are often subject to extortion because of government corruption, making them averse to owning property or improving it. This is especially damaging in a country that is very poor.

Although many economists see political instability and

government corruption as the leading causes of underdevelopment in Africa, some - most notably Jeffrey Sachs of Columbia University and the United Nations - believe the opposite. They argue that Africa is politically unstable because Africa is poor. And Africa's poverty stems from its extremely unfavorable geographic conditions -much of the continent is landlocked, hot, infested with tropical diseases, and cursed with poor soil.

Sachs, along with economists from the world health organization, has highlighted the importance of health problems in Africa. In poor countries, worker productivity is often severely hampered by malnutrition and disease. In particular, tropical diseases such as malaria can only be controlled with an effective public health infrastructure, something that is lacking in much of Africa.

Although the example of African countries represents a warning that long-run economic growth cannot be taken for granted, there are some signs of hope. Mauritius has developed a successful textile industry. Several African countries that are dependent on commodities such as coffee and oil have benefited from the recent sharp rise in the prices of commodities. And Ghana has managed to maintain an increase in real GDP per capita for several years now.

5, Are Economies Converging?

In the 1950s, much of Europe seemed quaint and backward to American visitors, and Japan seemed very poor. Today, a visitor to Paris or Tokyo sees a city that looks about as rich as New York. Although real GDP per capita is still somewhat higher in the United States, the differences in the standard of living among the United States, Europe, and Japan are relatively small.

Many economists have argued that this convergence in living standards is normall ; the convergence hypothesis says that relatively poor countries should have higher rates of growth of real GDP per capita than relatively rich countries. And if we look at today's relatively well - off countries, the convergence hypothesis seems to be true. Panel(a) of Figure 13 shows data for a number of today's wealthy economies. On the horizontal axis is real GDP per capita in 1955 ; on the vertical axis is growth rate of real GDP per capita from 1955 to 2001. There is a clear negative relationship. The United States was the richest country in this group in 1955 and the slowest rate of growth. Japan and Spain were the poorest countries in 1955 and had the fastest rate of growth. These data suggest that the convergence hypothesis is true.

Figure 13. Do Economies Converge ?

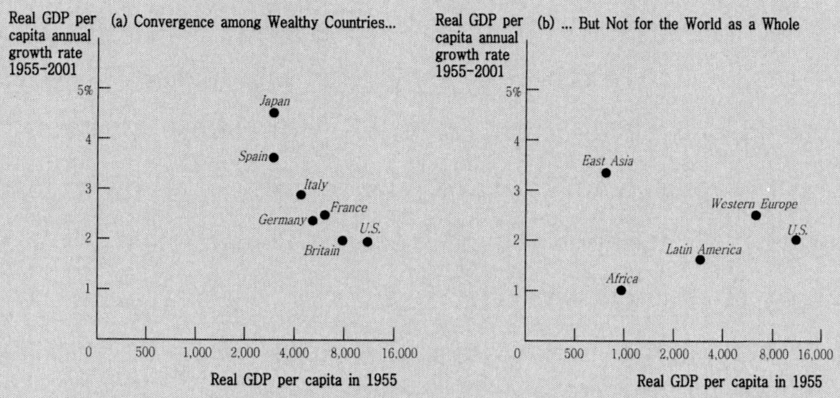

But economists who looked at similar data realized that these results depends on the countries selected. If you look at successful economies that have a high standard of living today, you find that real GDP per capita has converged. But looking across the world as whole, including countries that remain poor, there is little evidence of convergence. Panel(b) of Figure 13 illustrates this point using data for regions rather than individual countries. In 1955, East Asia and Africa were both very poor regions. Over the next 45 years, the East Asian regional economy grew quickly, as the convergence hypothesis would predicted, but the African regional economy grew very slowly. In 1955, Western Europe had subtantially higher real GDP per capita than Latin America. But, contrary to the hypothesis, the Western European regional economy grew more quickly, widening the gap between the regions

So is the convergence hypothesis all wrong ? No : economists still believe that countries with relatively low real GDP per capita tend to have higher rate of growth than countries with relatively high real GDP per capita, other things equal. But other things - education, infrastructure, rule of law, and so on - are often not equal. Statistical studies find that when you adjust for differences in these other factors, poorer countries do tend to have higher growth rates. This result is known as conditional convergence

Because other factors differ, there is no clear tendency toward convergence in the world economy as a whole. Western Europe, North America, and parts of Asia are becoming more similar in real GDP per capita, but the gap between these regions and the rest of the world is growing.

Appendix 2

The Stock Market and Residential Investment

- N. Gregory Mankiw, Macroeconomics
  Fifth ed., 2003, pp. 468-476

- D. Salvatore, International Economics
  Seventh ed., 2001, p. 369

- Olivier Blanchard, Macroeconomics
  Fourth ed. 2006, PP. 326-329, 481-484

확장적 금융정책으로 이자율을 하락시키면 주택수요와 주택담보대출이 증가하고 따라서 가계 부채가 증가한다. 우리 경제의 가계부채가 지속적으로 증가하는 중요한 요인 중에 하나가 이와 같은 이유 때문이다. 그러나 화폐는 장기에 중립적이다. 따라서 장기에는 가계 부채로 인해서 악순환의 위기에 빠질 수도 있다.

1, Tobin's q Theory

Many economists see a link between fluctuations in investment and fluctuations in the stock market. The term stock refers to the shares in the ownership of corporations, and the stock market is the market in which these shares are traded. Stock prices tend to be high when firms have many opportunities for profitable investment, because these profit opportunities mean higher future income for the shareholders. Thus, stock prices reflect the incentives to invest.

The Nobel - Prize - winning James Tobin proposed that firms base their investment decisions on the following ratio, which is now called Tobin's q :

$$q = \frac{\text{Market Value of Installed Capital}}{\text{Replacement Cost of Installed Capital}}$$

The numerator of Tobin's q is the value of the economy's capital as determined by the stock market. The denominator is the price of the capital if it were purchased today.

Tobin reasoned that net investment should depend on whether q is greater or less than 1. If q is greater than 1, then the stock market values installed capital at more than its replacement cost. In this case, managers can raise the market value of their firm's stock by buying more capital.

Although at first the q theory of investment may appear

quite different from the neoclassical model, in fact the two theories are closely related. To see the relationship, note that Tobin's q depends on current and future expected profits from installed capital. If the marginal product of capital exceeds the costs of capital, then firms are earning profit on their installed capital. These profits make the rental firms desirable to own, which raises the market value of these firm's stock, implying high value of q. Similarly, if the marginal product of capital falls short of the cost of capital, then firms are incurring losses on their installed capital, implying a low market value and a low value of q.

The advantage of Tobin's q as a measure of the incentive to invest is that it reflects the expected future profitability as well as the current profitablity. For example, suppose that Congress legislates a reduction in the corporate income tax beginning next year. This expected fall in the corporate tax means greater profits for the owners of capital. These higher expected profits raise the value of stock today, raise Tobin's q, and therefore encourage investment today. Thus, Tobin'q theory of investment emphasizes that investment decisions depend not only on current economic policies but also on policies expected to prevail in the future.

2, The Stock Market as an Economic Indicator

"The stock market has predicted nine out of the last five recessions." So goes Paul Samuelson's famous quip about the stock market's reliability as an economic indicator. The stock market is in fact quite volatile, and it can give false signals about the future of the economy. Yet one should not ignore the link between the stock market and the economy.

Why do stock prices and economic activity tend to fluctuate together? One reason is given by Tobin's q theory, together with the model of aggregate demand and aggregate supply. Suppose, for instance, that you observe a fall in stock prices. Because the replacement cost of capital is fairly stable, a fall in the stock market is usually associated with a fall in Tobin q. A fall in q reflects investors' pessimism about the current or future profitability of capital. This means that the investment function has shift inward : investment is lower at any given interest rate. As a result, the aggregate demand for good and services contracts, leading to lower output and employment.

There are two additional reasons why stock prices are associated with economic activity. First, because stock is part of household wealth, a fall in stock prices makes people poorer and thus depresses consumer spending, which also reduces aggregate demand. Second, a fall in stock prices might reflect bad news about technological progress and long-run economic growth. If so, this means that the natural rate of output - and thus aggregate supply - will be expanding more slowly in the future than was previously expected. Indeed, because the stock market often anticipates changes in real GDP, and because data on stock market are available more quickly than data on GDP, the stock market is a closely watched economic indicator.

3, Residential Investment

1) Housing Market

We begin by presenting a simple model of the housing market. There are two parts to the model. First, the market for existing stock of houses determines the equilibrium housing price. Second, the housing price determines the flow of residential investment.

Panel (a) of Figure 14 shows how the relative price of housing P_H/P is determined by the supply and demand for the existing stock of houses. At any point in time, the supply of houses is fixed. We represent this stock wth a vertical supply curve. The demand curve for houses slopes downward, because high prices cause people to live in smaller houses, to share residences, or sometimes even to become homeless. The price of housing adjusts to equilibrate supply and demand.

Figure 14. The Determination of Residential Investment

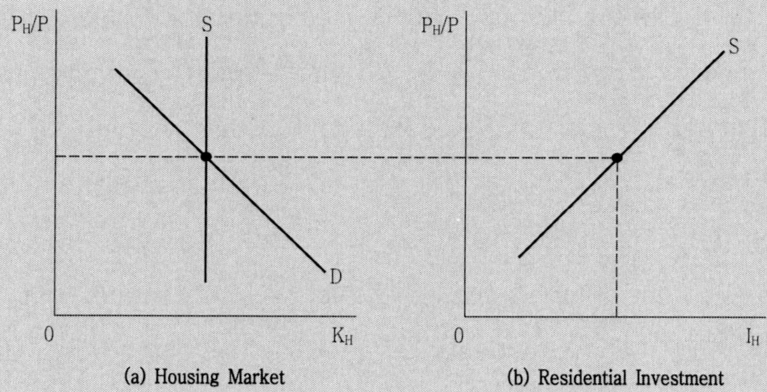

Panel (b) of Figure 14 shows how the relative price of housing determines the supply of new houses. Construction firms buy materials and hire labor to build houses, and then sell the house at the market price. Their costs depend on overall price level P (which reflects the cost of wood, bricks, plaster, etc), and their revenue depends on the price of houses P_H · The higher the relative price of housing, the greater the incentive to build houses, and the more houses are built. The flow of new houses - residential investment - therefore depends on the equilibrium price set in the market for existing houses.

This model of residential investment is similar to the q

theory of business fixed investment. According to the q theory, business fixed investment depends on the market price of installed capital relative to its replacement cost ; this relative price, in turn, depends on the expected profits from owning installed capital. According to this model of the housing merket, residential investment depends on the relative price of housing. The relative price of housing, in turn, depends on the demand for housing, which depends on the imputed rent that individuals expect to receive from their housing. Hence, the relative price of housing plays much the same role for residential investment as Tubin's q does for business fixed investment.

2) Changes in Housing Demand

When the demand for housing shifts, the equilibrium price of housing changes, and this change in turn affects residential investment.

The demand curve for housing can shift for various reasons, An economic boom raises national income and therefore the demand for housing. A large increase in the population, perhaps because of immigration, also raises the demand for housing. Panel (a) of Figure 15 shows that an expansionary shift in demand raises the equilibrium price.

Figure 15. An Increase in Housing Demand

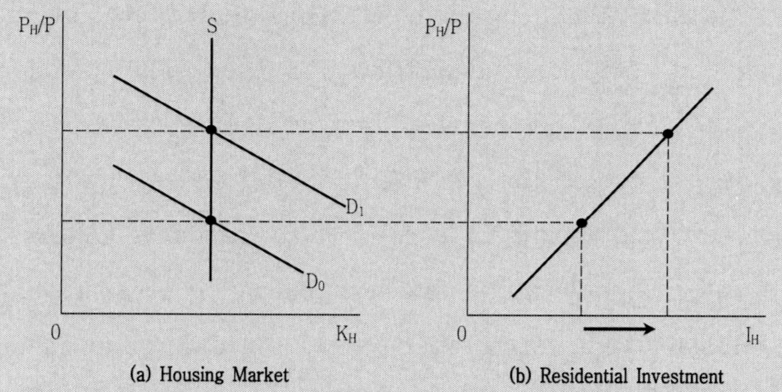

Panel (b) shows that the increase in the housing price increases residential investment.

One important determinant of housing demand is the real interest rate. Many people take out loans - mortgages - to buy their homes ; the interest rate is cost of the loan. Even the few people who do not have to borrow to purchase a home will respond to the interest rate, because the interest rate is the opportunity cost of holding their wealth in housing rather than putting it in a bank. A reduction in the interest rate thefore raises housing demand, housing prices, and residential investment.

3) The Crisis in Dynamic Asian Economies

The Dynamic Asian Economies(DAEs) and China grew at extremely high rates between 1980 and 1995. Then suddenly, in July 1997, Thailand plunged into a deep economic crisis that quickly spread to the other DAEs. The cause of the crisis was excessive borrowing of short - term funds in dollars and yens on international capital markets and using a great deal of these funds for real estate speculation and other unproductive investments. When local banks and firms were unable to repay their loans, foreign banks refused to extend new loans. Local banks then stopped making loans to local businesses, causing many of them to fail, and this plunged the nation into deep recession.

The GDP of Korea, Hong Kong, Thailand, and Malaysia declined by more than 5% between 1997 and 1998. Indonesia was even worse off with a decline in real GDP of nearly 15% and political unrest that toppled the Suharto government. Indeed, the growth of all developing countries and even that of industrial countries declined between 1997 and 1998. DAEs are now struggling to restructure their economies (especially the banking sector) so as to avoid future crises. In the meantime, growth resumed, but at lower rates than precrisis levels.

4. Stock Prices and Bubbles

Do all movements in stock prices come from news about future devidends or interest rates?

Many economists doubt it. They point to Black October in 1929, when the U.S stock market fell by 23% in two days, and to October 19, 1987, when the Dow Jones index fell by 22.6% in a single day. They point to the amazing rise in Japanese stock prices in the 1980s, followed by a sharp fall in the 1990s. As we can see in Figure 16, the Nikkei index increased from around 13,000 in 1985 to around 35,000 in 1989, only to decline back to around 16,000 in 1992. In each of these cases, they point to a lack of obvious news, or at least of news important enough to cause such enormous movements.

Figure 16. The Japanese Stock Market Index since 1980

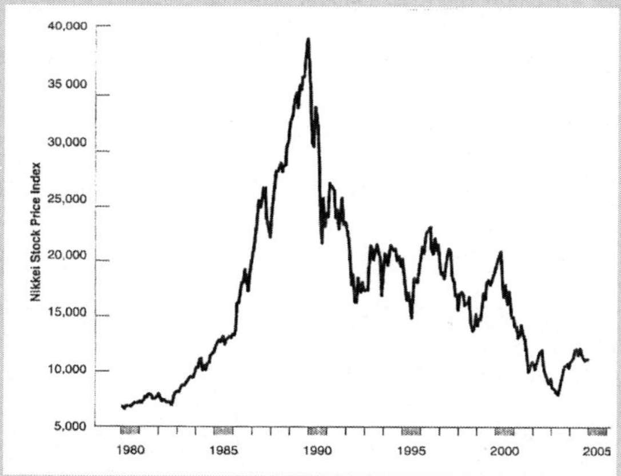

Instead, they argue that stock prices are not always equal to their fundamental value, defined as the present value of expected dividends, and that stocks are sometimes underpriced or overpriced. Overpricing eventually comes to an end, sometimes with a crash as in October 1929, or with a long slide as in the case of the Nikkei index.

Under what conditions can such mispricing occur? The surprising answer is that it can occur even when investors are rational, and when arbitrage holds.

To see why, consider the case of a truly worthless stock. That is, the stock of a company that all financial investors know will never make profits and will never pay dividends. The fundamental value of such a stock is equal to zero.

Might you, nevertheless, be willing to pay a positive price for this stock?

Maybe. you might if you expect the price at which you can sell the stock next year to be higher than this year's price. And the same applies to a buyer next year. He may well be willing to buy at a high price if he expects to sell at an even higher price in the following year.

This process suggests that stock prices may increase just because investors expect them to. Such movements in stock prices are called rational speculative bubbles.

Financial investors might well be behaving rationally as the bubble inflates. Even those investors who hold the stock at the time of the crash, and therefore sustain a large loss, may also have been rational. They may have realized there was a chance of a crash, but also a chance that the bubble would continue, and they could sell at an even higher price.

To make things simple, our example assumed the stock to be fundamentally worthless. But the argument is general and applies to stocks with a positive fundamental value as well. People might be willing to pay more than the fundamental value of a stock if they expect its price to further increase in the future. And the same argument applies to other assets, such as housing, gold, and paintings

Are all deviations from fundamental values in financial markets rational bubbles?

Probably not. The fact is that many financial investors are not rational.

An increase in stock prices in the past, say due to a succession of good news, often creates excessive optimism. If investors simply extrapolate from past returns to predict future returns, a stock may become "hot"(high priced) for no reason other than its price has increased in the past. Such deviations of stock prices from their fundamental value are called fads. We are all aware of fads outside of the stock market ; there are good reasons to believe they exist in the stock market as well.

Figure 17, Standard and Poor's Stock Price Index, in Real Terms since 1980

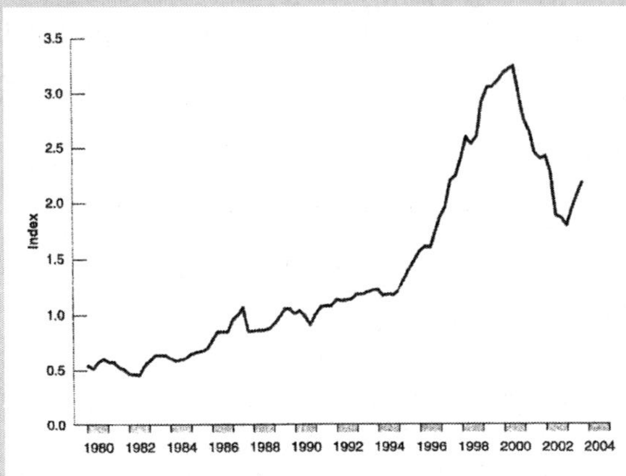

Let's now go back to the facts we can see in figure 17, and ask : Was the large increase in the stock market in 1990s due to fundamentals or to a bubble?

After the 1990-1991 recession, the U.S. economy went through a long expansion - an expansion lasting much longer than most economists and financial investors had anticipated.

With the long expansion came high profits and high dividends - much higher than had been expected. The rate of technological progress increased, promising higher growth and higher profits for firms in the future. The natural rate of unemployment decreased, allowing the Fed to keep interest rates low for most of the decade. This good news should have led to higher than expected stock prices.

But did this good news justify the tripling of the stock price index that actually occurred? At the time, many economists were - and still are - doubtful. They point to the evolution of the Nasdaq, an index that includes mostly high-tech stocks. The Nasdaq went from 400 in 1990 to 3,900 in 2000, only to fall back to 1,350 in 2003. They point to the increasing number of individuals who would buy stocks on the internet, without knowing anything about the stock itself, only in anticipation of selling it the next day at a higher price.

Indeed, in 1997, Alan Greenspan spoke of irrational exuberance, warning that stock prices were probably too high.

Another way of looking at the question is to ask : Was the sharp decline of the stock market in the early 2000s associated with bad news on fundamentals, or the bursting of a bubble? Most of the evidence points primarily to the bursting of a bubble. The news on productivity growth has continued to be good.

Under this interpretation, some of the increase in 1990s was indeed unjustified, and this is what led to the sharp correction in the early 2000s. After this correction, however, the level of index still stood at more than twice its value in 1990, reflecting the improvement in fundamentals

The decline in the stock market was one of the factors behind the 2001 recession. Most economists also believe that the stock market crash of 1929 was one of the sources of the Great Depression, and that the large decline in the Nikkei is one of the causes of the long Japanese slump in the 1990s.

The 1980s were associated with a stock market boom in Japan. The Nikkei index, a broad index of Japanese stock prices, increased from 7,000 in 1980 to 35,000 at the end of 1989 - a fivefold increase. Then, within 2 years, the index fell sharply - down to 16,000 at the end of 1992. Since then, it has declined further, and at the end of 2003, it stood slightly above 10,000, less than one - third of its value at the peak.

Why did the Nikkei rise so much in the 1980s and then fall so quickly in the early 1990s? There can be two reasons for a stock price to increase :

1) A change in the fundamental value of the stock price, coming, for example, from an increase in current or future expected dividends. Knowing that the stock will pay higher dividends either now or in the future, investors are willing to pay more for the stock today. Consequently its price goes up.

2) A speculative bubble. Investors buy at a higher price simple because they expect the price to go even higher in the future.

While the stock price index increased in the 1980s, the dividends remained flat. This is not necessarily proof that the increase in the Nikkei was a bubble. Investors might have expected large increases in future dividends, even if current dividends were not increasing. But it strongly suggests that the increase in the Nikkei had a large bubble component, and that the latter fall was largely a bursting of that bubble.

Whatever its origin, the rapid fall in the stock prices had a major impact on spending and, in turn, a big impact on output. Investment, which had been very strong during the rise of the Nikkei, callapsed. In contrast to the Great Depression, consumption was less affected. But the strength in consumption was not enough to avoid a sharp decline in total spending and in GDP growth, from 6.5% in 1989 to 0.2% in 1993

From the end of World War II to the beginning of the 1990s, Japanese economic performance was spectacular. From 1950 to 1973, the average growth rate was 7.4% per year. As in other OECD countries, the average growth rate decreased after 1973. But, from 1973 to 1991, it was still a very respectable 4% per year, a rate higher than in most other OECD countries. As a result of this growth, Japanese output per capita, which was equal to only 22% of the U.S. level in 1950, had climbed to 84% of the U.S. level in 1990

This growth came to an abrupt end in the early 1990s. From 1992 to 2002, the growth rate was either positive and small, or nagative. The average growth rate was 1% - far below what it had been in earlier decades. This long period of low growth is what is called the Japanese slump. This slump was obviously not as sharp and as deep as the Great Depression, but it was still substantial. Think of it this way. If average output growth between 1992 and 2002 had been the same as during 1973 to 1991, output in Japan would have been roughly 30% higher in 2002 than it actually was.

Since 2003, there are signs that the slump may be coming to an end. Output growth was higher in 2003 and is projected to be higher again in 2004. Previous hopes of a recovery, in 1996 and again in 2000, were dashed when higher growth rates did not last. This time, economists are a bit more optimistic. In the best of cases, however, it will still take many years for the Japanese economy to return to normal.

Low output growth has led to a steady increase in unemployment. The unemployment rate has increased from 2.1% in 1990 to 5.0% in 2004. But 5.0% is still lower than the average unemployment rate in the United States over the last 40 years, and it is a rate that many European countries can only dream of achieving. This conclusion would be wrong, however. An unemployment rate of 5% in Japan is the sign of an extremely depressed labor market

To see why, go back to the discussion of the organization of firms and of the labor market in Japan. Japanes firms offer substantial employment protection to their workers. So, when Japanese firms experience a decrease in production, they tend to keep their workers, leading to a small effect of the decrease in output on employment. As a result, unemployment does not rise much.

A useful way to think about the evolution of unemployment in Japan is in terms of Okun's law. In the United States, the Okun coefficient is equal to 0.4. A decrease in the growth rate of 1% for 1 year leads to an increase in the unemployment rate of 0.4%. In Japan, the Okun coefficient is equal to 0.1. A decrease in the growth rate of 1% for 1 year leads to an increase in the unemployment rate of only 0.1%.

As cumulative output growth in Japan since 1992 has been roughly about 30% below normal, this has resulted in an increase in the unemployment rate of 0.1 × 30% = 3%. In the United States, the same shortfall in growth would have led to an increase in unemployment of 0.4 × 30% = 12%, a much larger increase.

Low growth and high unemployment (by Japanese standards) have led to a steady fall in the inflation rate in Japan over time. The inflation rate was already low at the start of the 1990s. Since 1995, inflation has turned into deflation, something that had not been observed in OECD countries since the Great Depression. Despite higher output growth since 2003, unemployment is still high in Japan, and so deflation continues.

Appendix 3

Exchange Rate Crises under Fixed Exchange Rates

Olivier Blanchard, Macroeconomics,
Fourth ed. 2006, PP. 447 - 449

Suppose a country is operating under a fixed exchange rate. Suppose also that financial investors start believing there may soon be an exchange rate adjustment - either a devaluation or a shift to a flexible exchange rate regime accompanied by a depreciation.

We just saw why this might be the case :

1) The real exchange rate may be too high. Or, put another way, the domestic currency may be overvalued. In this case, a real depreciation is called for. While this could be achieved in the medium run without a devaluation, financial investors may conclude that the government will take the quickest way out- and devalue.

Such an overvaluation often happens in countries that peg their nominal exchange rate to a country with lower inflation. Higher relative inflation implies a steadily increasing price of domestic goods relative to foreign goods, a steady real appreciation, and so a steady worsening of the trade position.

As time passes, the need for an adjustment of the real exchange rate increases, and financial investors become more and more nervous.

2) Internal condition may call for a decrease in the domestic interest rate. A decrease in the domestic interest rate cannot be achieved under fixed exchange rate. But it can be achieved if the country is willing to shift to a flexible exchange rate regime. If a country lets the exchange rate

float and then decreases its domestic interest rate, this will trigger a decrease in the nominal exchange rate - a nominal depreciation.

As soon as financial markets believe a devaluation may be coming, then to maintain the exchange rate requires an increase, often a large one, in the domestic interest rate. To see this, return to the interest - parity condition :

$$i_t = i_t^* - \frac{(E_{t+1}^e - E_t)}{E_t}$$

We interpreted this equation as a relation between the 1-year domestic and foreign nominal interest rates, the current exchange rate, and the expected exchange rate a year hence. But the choice of 1 year as the period was arbitrary. The relation holds over a day, a week, a month. If financial markets expect the exchange rate to be 2% lower a month from now, they will hold domestic bonds only if the 1-month domestic interest rate exceeds the 1-month foreign interest rate by 2% (or, if we express interest rates at an annual rate, the domestic interest rate exceeds the foreign interest rate by 2% ×12 = 24%)

Under fixed exchange rates, the current exchange rate E_t is set at some level, say $E_t = \bar{E}$. If markets expect the parity will be maintained over the period, then $E_{t+1}^e = \bar{E}$, and the interest-parity condition simply states that the domestic and the foreign interest rates must be equal.

Suppose, however, participants in financial markets start anticipating a devaluation - a decrease in the exchange rate. Suppose they believe that, over the coming month, there is a 75% chance the parity will be maintained and a 25% chance there will be a 20% devaluation. The term $(E^e_{t+1} - E_t)/E_t$ in the interest - parity equation, which we assumed equal to zero earlier, now equals 0.75×0% +0.25×(-20%)=-5%(a 75% chance of no change plus a 25% chance of a devaluation of 20%). This implies that if the central bank wants to maintain the existing parity, it must now offer a monthly interest rate 5% higher than before - 60% higher at an annual rate (12×5%). 60% is the interest differential needed to convince investors to hold domestic bonds rather than foreign bonds!

What, then, are the choices confronting the government and the central bank?

1) First, the government and the central bank can try to convince markets they have no intention of devaluing. This is always the first line of defense. Communiqués are issued, and prime ministers go on TV to reiterate their absolute commitment to the existing parity.

But words are cheap, and they rarely convince financial investors.

2) Second, the central bank can increase the interest rate, but by less than would be needed to satisfy - in our example, by less than 60%. Although domestic interest rates are high,

they are not high enough to fully compensate for the perceived risk of devaluation.

This action typically leads to a large capital outflow, as financial investors still prefer to get out of domestic bonds into foreign bonds. This implies selling domestic bonds, getting the proceeds in domestic currency, going to the foreign exchange market to sell domestic currency for foreign currency, and then buying foreign bonds. If the central bank did not intervene in the foreign-exchange market, the large sales of domestic currency for foreign currency would lead to a depreciation. If it wants to maintain the exchage rate, the central bank must therefore stand ready to buy domestic currency and sell foreign currency at the current exchange rate. In doing so, it often loses most of its reserves of foreign currency.

3) Eventually - after a few hours or a few weeks - the choice for the central bank become either to increase the interest rate enough to satisfy or to validate the market's expectation and devalue. Setting a very high short term domestic interest rate can have a devastating effect on demand and on output. This course of action makes sense only if (1) the perceived probability of a devaluation is small, so the interest rate does not have to be too high, and (2) the government believes markets will soon become convinced that

no devaluation is coming, allowing domestic interest rates to decrease. Otherwise, the only option is to devalue. All these steps were very much in evidence during the exchange rate crisis that affected much of western Europe in 1992.

To summarize : Expectations that a devaluation may be coming can trigger an exchange rate crisis. Faced with such expections, the government has two options :

1. Give in and devalue.

2. Fight and maintain the parity, at the cost of very high interest rates and a potential recession. Fighting may not work anyway. The recession may force the government to change policy later on or force the government out of office.

An interesting twist here is that a devaluation may happen even if the belief that a devaluation was coming was initially groundless. Even if the government initially had no intention of devaluing, it may be forced to devalue if financial markets believe that it will devalue

The cost of maintaining the parity would be a long period of high interest rates and a recession ; the government prefers to devalue instead.

Appendix 4

Inflation and Monetary Policy

이 입증자료와 미국의 금융정책에서 알 수 있는 바와 같이 아직까지도 세계경제는 디스인플레이션시대에 있다고 할 수 있다.

- N. Gregory Mankiw, Macroecomomics, Fifth ed., 2003, pp. 359-367, 370-371
- Paul A. Samuelson and William D. Nordhous Economics, Fourteenth ed., 1992, PP.606-615
- Olivier Blanchard, Macroeconomics, Fourth ed., 2006, PP.539-545
- P. Krugman and R. Wells, Macroeconomics First ed., 2006, PP.385-388, P.425

1. The Phillips Curve Equation

The Phillips curve in its modern form states that the inflation rate depends on three forces :

1) Expected inflation (π^e)

2) The deviation of unemployment from the natural rate, called cyclical unemployment ($u - u_n$)

3) Supply shocks (V)

The three forces are expressed in the following equation:

$$\pi = \pi^e - \beta(u - u_n) + V$$

where β is a parameter measuring the response of inflation to the cyclical unemployment.

Notice that there is a minus sign before the cyclical unemployment term : high unemployment tends to reduce inflation. This equation summarizes the relationship between inflation and unemployment

To make the Phillips curve useful for analyzing the choices facing policymakers, we need to say what determines expected inflation. A simple and often plausible assumption is that people form their expectations of inflation on recently observed inflation. This assumption is called adaptive expectations. For example, suppose that people expect prices to rise this year at the same rate as they did last year. Then expected inflation π^e equals last year's inflation π_{-1} :

$$\pi^e = \pi_{-1}$$

In this case, we can write the phillips curve as

$$\pi = \pi_{-1} - \beta(u - u_n) + V$$

which states that inflation depends on past inflation, cyclical unemployment, and a supply shock.

When the phillips curve is written in this form, the natural rate of unemployment is sometimes called the Non-Accelerating Inflation Rate of Unemployment, or NAIRU.

The first term in this form of the Phillips curve, π_{-1}, implies that inflation has inertia. That is, like an object moving through space, inflation keeps going unless something acts to stop it. In particular, if unemployment is at the NAIRU and if there are no supply shock, the continued rise in price level neither speeds up nor slows down. This inertia arises because past inflation influences expectations of future inflation and because these expectations influence the wages and prices that people set.

In the model of aggreate supply and aggregate demand, inflaion inertia is interpreted as persistent upward shifts in both the aggregate supply curve and the aggregate demand curve. Consider first aggregate supply. If prices have been rising quickly, people will expect them to continue to rise quickly. Because the position of the short-run aggregate supply curve depends on the expected price level, the short-run aggregate supply curve will shift upward over time, It will continue to shift upward until some event, such as a recession or a supply shock, changes inflation and thereby changes expectations of inflation.

The aggregate demand curve must also shift upward to confirm the expectations of inflation. Most often, the continued rise in aggregate demand is caused by persistent growth in the money supply. If the Fed suddenly halted money growth, aggregate demand would stabilize, and the upward shift in aggreate supply would cause a recession. The high unemployment in the recession would reduce inflation and expected inflation, causing inflation inertia to subside

2. Inflation Expectation and the Short-Run Phillips Curve

The expected rate of inflation is the rate of inflation that employers and workers expect in the near future. One of the crucial discoveries of modern macroeconomics is that the expected rate of inflation affects the short-run trade-off between unemployment and inflation.

Why does expected inflation affect the short-run Phillips curve? The answer lies in the part with the fact that wages are sticky. Put yourself in the position of a worker or employer about to sign a contract setting the worker's wages over the next year. For a number of reasons, the wage rate they agree to will be higher if everyone expects high inflation (including rising wages) than if everyone expects prices to be stable. The worker will want a wage rate that takes into account future declines in the purchasing power of earnings. She or he will also want a wage rate that won't fall behind the wages of other workers. And the employers will be more willing to agree to a wage increase now if hiring workers later will be even more expensive. Also, rising prices will make paying a higher wage rate more affordable because the employer's output will sell for more.

For these reasons, an increase in expected inflation shifts the short-run Phillips curve upward : the actual rate of inflation at any given unemployment rate is higher when the expected inflation rate is higher. In fact, macroeconomists believe that the relationship between expected inflation and actual inflation is one-to-one. That is, when the expected inflation rate increases, the actual inflation rate at any given unemployment rate will increase by the same amount. When the expected inflation rate falls, the actual inflation rate at any given level of unemployment will fall by the same amount

Figure 18. Expected Inflation and the Short-Run Phillips Curve

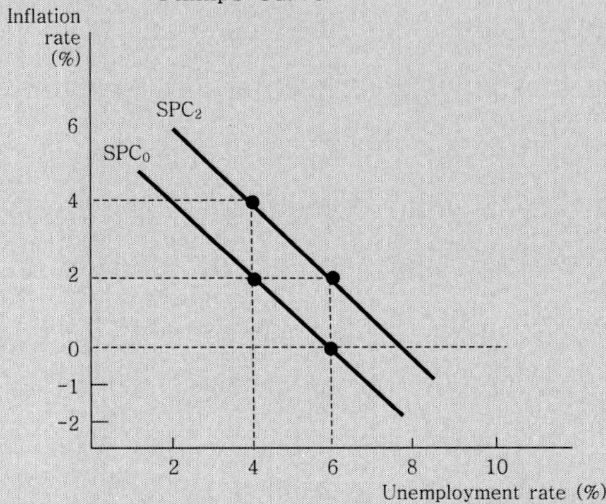

Figure 18 shows how the expected rate of inflation affects the short-run Phillips curve.

First, suppose that the expected rate of inflation is 0% : people expect 0% inflation in the near future. SPC_0 is the short-run Phillips curve when the public expects 0% inflation. According to SPC_0, the actual inflation rate will be 0% if the unemployment rate is 6% ; it will be 2% if the unemployment rate is 4%.

Alternatively, suppose the expected rate of inflation is 2%. In that case, employers and workers will build this expectation into wages and prices : at any given unemployment rate, the actual inflation rate will be 2% higher than it would be if people expected 0% inflation. SPC_2, which shows the Phillips curve when the expected inflation rate is 2%, is SPC_0 shifted upward by 2% at every level of unemployment. According to SPC_2, the actual inflation rate will be 2% if the unemployment rate is 6% ; it will be 4% if the unemployment rate is 4%.

What determines the expected rate of inflation? In general, people base their expectations about inflation on experience. If the inflation rate hovered around 0% in the last few years, people will expect it to be around 0% in the near future. But if the inflation rate has averaged around 5% lately, people will expect inflation to be around 5% in the near future.

Since expected inflation is an important part of the modern short-run Phillips curve discussion, you might wonder why it was not in the original formulation of the Phillips curve. But think back to what we said about the early 1960s : at that point, people were accustomed to low inflation rates and reasonably expected that future inflation rates would also be modest. It was only after 1965 that persistent inflation became a fact of life.

So it was only at that point that it became clear that expected inflation would play an important role in price-setting.

3. The Long-Run Phillips Curve

Figure 19 reproduces the two short-run Phillips curves from figure 18, SPC_0 and SPC_2. It also adds an additional short-run Phillips curve, SPC_4, representing a 4% expected rate of inflation. We'll explain why these are short-run curve in a moment, and we'll also explain the significance of the vertical long-run Phillips curve, LPC.

Suppose that the economy has, in the past, had a 0% inflation rate. In that case the current short-run Phillips curve will reflect a 0% expected inflation rate, so it will be SPC_0. If the unemployment rate is 6%, the actual inflation rate will be 0%.

Also suppose that policy makers try to trade off lower unemployment for a higher rate of inflation. They use monetary policy, fiscal policy, or both to drive the unemployment rate down to 4%. This puts the economy at point A on SPC_0 leading to an actual inflation rate of 2%.

Over time, the public will come to expect a 2% inflation rate. This will shift the short-run Phillip curve to SPC_2. Now, when the unemployment rate is 6%, the actual inflation rate will be 2%. Given this new short-run Phillips curve, keeping the unemployment rate at 4% will lead to a 4% actual inflation rate - point B on SPC_2 - rather than 2%

Figure 19. The NAIRU and the Long-Run Phillips Curve

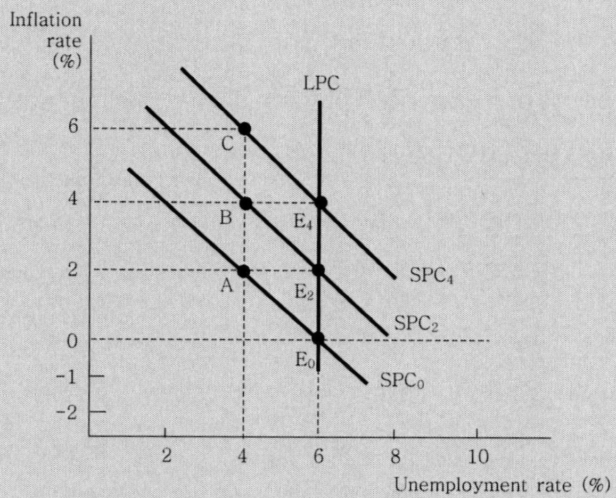

Eventually, this 4% inflation rate gets built into expectations, and the short-run Phillips curve shifts upward again, to SPC_4. To keep the unemployment rate at 4% would now require accepting a 6% actual inflation rate (point C of SPC_4), and so on. In short, a persistent attempt to trade off lower unemployment for higher inflation leads to accelerating inflation over time.

To avoid accelerating inflation over time, the unemployment rate must be high enough so that the actual rate of inflation matches the expected rate of inflation. This is situation at E_0 on SPC_0 : when the expectred inflation rate is 0% and the unemployment rate is 6%, the actual inflation rate is 0%. It is also the situation at E_2 on SPC_2: when the expected inflation rate is 2% and the unemployment rate is 6%, the actual inflation rate is 2%. And it is the situation at E_4 on SPC_4 : when the expected inflation rate is 4% and the unemployment rate is 6%, the actual inflation rate is 4%

The unemployment rate at which inflation does not change over time - 6% in Figure 19 - is known as the nonaccelerating inflation rate of unemployment, or NAIRU for short. Unemployment rates below the NAIRU lead to ever-accelerating inflation and cannot be maintained. Most economists believe that there is a NAIRU and that there is no long-run trade-off between unemployment and inflation.

We can now explain the significance of the vertical line LPC. It is the long-run Phillips curve, the relationship between unemployment and inflation in the long run, after expectations of inflation have had time to adjust to experience. It is vertical because any unemployment rate below the NAIRU leads to ever accelerating inflation and any unemployment rate above the NAIRU leads to decelerating inflation. In other words, it shows that an unemployment rate below the NAIRU cannot be maintained in the long run.

The NAIRU is another name for the natural rate. The level of unemployment the economy "needs" in order to avoid accelerating inflation is equal to the sum of frictional unemployment plus structural unemployment. Growing out of theoretical work of Edmund Phelps and Milton Friedman, and tested by scores of econometricians, the natural-rate theory implies that the long-run Phillips curve is vertical. In an economy concerned with preventing high inflation rates, the natural rate of unemployment is the lowest level that can be sustained ; it thus represents the highest sustainable level of employment and corresponds to a nation's potential output.

What would happen if there were either demand or cost shocks? At very low unemployment, such as that during the Vietnam war, inflation will be pushed above its inertial rate as we move along the short-run Phillips curve. By contrast, if unemployment rises to levels far in excess of the natural rate, as occurred in the early 1980s, inflation will decline below its inertial rate as we move down the short-run Phillips curve

But the story does not end here. Once actual inflation rises above its inertial or expected level, people begin to adjust to the new level of inflation and to expect higher inflation. The inertial rate of inflation then adjusts to the new reality. And the short-run Phillips curve shifts.

Rapid growth and low unemployment during the Vietnam war led to the bidding up of prices and wages - a demand shock occurred. Actual inflation rose, and inertial inflation quickly followed suit.

Oil-price shocks in 1973 and 1979 raised actual inflation, and again inertial inflation followed. In 1980-1982, however, policymakers decided to pay almost any price in a crusade against inflation. The subsequent recession drove down actual inflation, and inertial inflation declined sharply in the late 1980s.

We have seen that when the unemployment rate diverges from the natural rate of unemployment, the inflation rate will tend to change. What happens if the gap persists? For example, say that the natural rate is 6%, while the actual unemployment rate is 4%. Because of the gap, inflation will tend to rise from year to year. Inflation might be 6% in the first year, and might continue to move upward thereafter.

When would this upward spiral stop? According to the natural-rate theory, it will stop only when unemployment moves back to its natural rate. Put differently, as long as unemployment is below the natural rate, inflation will tend to increase.

The opposite behavior will be seen at high unemployment. In that case, inflation will tend to fall as long as unemployment is above the natural rate

Only when unemployment is at the natural rate will inflation stabilize ; only then will inflation - at whatever is its inertial rate - tend neither to increase nor to decrease.

According to the natural -rate theory, the only level of unemployment consistent with a stable inflation rate is the natural rate of unemployment. The long-run Phillips curve must, in this theory, be drawn as a vertical line at the natural unemployment rate.

The natural-rate theory of inflation has two important implications for economy policy.

First, it implies that there is a minimum level of unemployment that an economy can sustain in the long run. According to this view, a nation cannot push unemployment below the natural rate for long without igniting an upward spiral of wage and price inflation.

Second, a nation may be able to ride the short-run Phillips curve. An expansionist president can drive the unemployment rate below the natural rate and the nation can temporarily enjoy low unemployment, but at the expense of rising inflation. Conversely, when a nation thinks that its inertial inflation rate is too high, as was the case in 1979-1982, it can steel itself for a period of austerity, induce a recession, and thereby reduce inflation.

4. Anti-inflation Policy

1) How long is the long run?

The natural rate theory holds that the Phillips curve is vertical in the long run. Just how long is the long run for this purpose? The length of time that it takes the economy to adjust fully to a shock is not precisely known. Recent studies suggest that full adjustment takes at least 5 years, and some studies conclude that the Phillips curve would not become vertical until more than a decade. These analyses indicate that it takes a long time for expectations to adjust, for labor and other long-term contracts to be renegotiated, and for all these effects to percolate through the economy. In addition, the length of time it takes for the economy to adjust probably depends on the type and novelty of the shock.

2) How much does it cost to reduce inflation?

Our analysis suggests that a nation can reduce the inertial rate of inflation by reducing output and raising unemployment for a time. But in weighing anti-inflation policies, policymakers may want to know just how much it costs to squeeze inflation out of the economy. How costly is disinflation, the policy of lowering the rate of inflation? This is equivalent to asking about the shape of the short-run Phillips curve. If the Phillips curve is relatively flat, reducing inflation will require a big increase in unemployment ; if the Phillips curve is steep, a small rise in unemployment will bring down inflation quickly and relatively painlessly.

3) Disinflation and the sacrifice ratio

Imagine an economy in which unemployment is at its natural rate and inflation is running at 6%. What would happen to unemployment and ouput if the central bank pursued a policy to reduce inflation from 6% to 2%?

The Phillips curve shows that in the absence of a beneficial supply shock, lowering inflation requires a period of high unemployment and reduced output. But by how much and for how long would unemployment need to rise above the natural rate? Before deciding whether to reduce inflation, policymakers must know how much output would be lost during the transition to lower inflation, The cost can then be compared with the benefits of lower inflation.

Much research has used the available data to examine the Phillips curve quantitatively.

The results of these studies are often summarized in a number called the sacrifice ratio, the percentage of a year's real GDP that must be forgone to reduce inflation by 1%. Although estimates of the sacrifice ratio vary substantially, a typical estimate is about 5 : for every percentage point that inflation is to fall, 5% of one year's GDP must be sacrificed.

We can also express the sacrifice ratio in terms of

unemployment. Okun's law says that a change of 1% in the unemployment rate translated into a change of 2% in GDP.

Therefore, reducing inflation by 1% requires about 2.5% of cyclical unemployment.

We can use the sacrifice ratio to estimate by how much and for how long unemployment must rise to reduce inflation. If reducing inflation by 1% requires a sacrifice of 5% of a year's GDP, reducing inflation by 4% requires a sacrifice of 20% of a year's GDP. Equivalently, this reduction in inflation requires a sacrifice of 10% of cyclical unemployment.

This disinflation could take various forms, each totaling the same sacrifice of 20% of a year's GDP. For example, a rapid disinflation would lower output by 10% for 2 years : this is sometimes called the cold-turkey solution to inflation.

A moderate disinflation would lower output by 5% for 4 years. An even more gradual disinflation would depress output by 2% for a decade.

5. Inflation and Nominal Money Growth

Until the 1990's the design of monetary policy typically centered around nominal money growth. Central banks chose a nominal money growth target for the medium run. And they thought about short-run monetary policy in terms of deviations of nominal money growth from that target. In the past decade, however, this design has evolved. Most central banks have adopted an inflation rate target rather than a nominal money growth rate target. And they think about short-run monetary policy in terms of movements in the nominal interest rate rather than in terms of movement in the rate of nominal money growth. Let's first look at what they did earlier, before turning to what they do now.

Until the 1990's monetary policy, in the Untied States and in other OECD countries, was typically conducted as follows:

1) The central bank chose a target rate for nominal money growth corresponding to the inflation rate it wanted to achieve in the medium run.

If, for example, it wanted to achieve an inflation rate of 4% and the normal rate of growth of output (the rate of growth implied by the rate of technological progress and the rate of population growth) was 3%, the central bank chose a target rate of nominal money growth of 7%.

2) In the short run, the central bank allowed for deviations of nominal money growth from the target, If, for example, the economy was in a recession, the central bank increased nominal money growth above the target value, so as to allow for a decrease in the interest rate and a faster recovery of output. In an expansion, it might do the reverse, so as to

slow output growth.

3) To communicate to the public both what it wanted to achieve in the medium run and what it intended to do in the short run, the central bank announced a range for the rate of nominal money growth it intended to achieve. Sometimes, this range was presented as a commitment from the central bank ; sometimes, it was presented simply as a forecast rather than as a commitment.

Over time, central banks became disenchanted with this way of conducting monetary policy. Let's now see why.

The design of monetary policy around nominal money growth is based on the assumption that there is close relation between inflation and nominal money growth in the medium run.

The problem is that, in practice, this relation is not very tight. If nominal money growth is high, inflation will also be high ; and if nominal money growth is low, inflation will be low. But the relation is not tight enough that, by choosing a rate of nominal money growth, the central bank can achieve precisely its desired rate of inflation, not even in the medium run.

The relation between inflation and nominal money growth is shown in Figure 20, which plots 10-year averages of the inflation rate against 10-year averages of the growth rate of the money stock since 1970 to 2003, so the numbers for inflation and for money growth for 2000, for example, are the average inflation rate and the average growth rate of money from 1991 to 2000. The inflation rate is constructed using the CPI as the price index. The growth rate of nominal money is constructed using M1 as the measure for the money stock, The reason for using 10-year averages should be clear. In the short run, changes in nominal money growth affect mostly output, not inflation. It is only in the medium run that a rlation between nominal money growth and inflation should emerge. Taking 10-year averages of both nominal money growth and inflation is a way of detecting such a medium run relation.

Figure 20 shows that, for the Unted States since 1970, the relation between M1 growth and inflation has not been very tight.

Figure 20, Inflation and Nominal Money Growth (10-year averages since 1970)

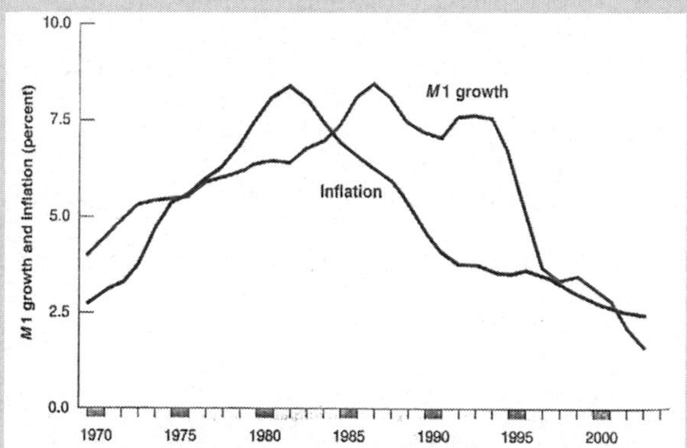

True, both went up at the beginning of the period, and both have come down since. But note how inflation started declining in the early 1980s, while nominal money growth remained high for another decade and came down only in the 1990s. Average inflation from 1981 to 1990 was down to 4%, while average money growth over the same peorid was still runing at 7.5%. Since 2000, the situation has been the reverse: Average money growth is now lower than average inflation.

Why is the relation between M1 growth and inflation not tighter? The answer is because of shifts in the demand for money. An example will help. Suppose, as the result of the introduction of credit cards, people decide to hold only half the amount of money they held before ; in other words, the real demand for money decreases by half. In the medium run, the real money stock must also decreases by half. For a given nominal money stock, the price level must double. Even if the nominal money stock was to remain constant, there would still be a period of inflation as the price level doubles. During this period, there will be no tight relation between nominal money growth and inflation.

Frequent and large shifts in money demand created serious problems for central banks.

They found themselves torn between trying to keep a

stable target for money growth and staying within announced bands, or adjusting to shifts in money demand. Starting in the early 1990's, a dramatic rethinking of monetary policy took place, based on inflation targeting rather than on money growth targeting, and the use of interest rate rules. Let's look at the way monetary policy is conducted today.

6. Inflation Targeting

In many countries, central banks have defined as their primary goal the achievement of a low inflation rate, both in the short run and in the medium run. This is known as inflation targeting. First to adopt inflation targeting was New Zealand in 1990, which set a target range for inflation of 0% to 2%, later extended to 0% to 3%. Next was Canada in 1991, setting a target range for inflation of 0% to 2%. Since then, some form of inflation targeting has been adopted by, among others, the United Kingdom, Sweden, Israel, Chile, Brazil, Poland, and Hungary.

Trying to achieve a given inflation target in the medium run would seem, and indeed is, a clear improvement over trying to achieve a nominal money growth target.

After all, in the medium run, the primary goal of monetary policy is to achieve a given rate of inflation. Better to have an inflation rate as the target than a nominal money growth target, which, as you have seen, may not lead to the desired rate of inflation.

Trying to achieve a given inflation target in the short run would appear to be much more controversial. Focusing exclusively on inflation would seem to eliminate any role monetary policy could play to reduce output fluctuations. But, in fact, this is not the case. To see why, return to the Phillips curve relation between inflation, π_t, lagged inflation, π_{t-1}, and the deviation of the unemployment rate u_t from the natural rate of unemployment, u_n :

$$\pi_t = \pi_{t-1} - \alpha(u_t - u_n)$$

Let the inflation rate target be $\pi*$. Suppose the central bank could achieve its inflation target exactly in every period. Then, the relation would become

$$\pi^* = \pi^* - \alpha(u_t - u_n)$$

The unemployment rate u_t would always equal u_n, the natural rate of unemployment ; by implication, output would always be equal to the natural level of output. In effect, inflation targeting would lead the central bank to act in such a way as to eliminate all deviations of output from its natural level.

The intuition ; If the central bank saw that an adverse demand shock was going to lead to a recession, it would know that absent a monetary expansion, the economy would experience a decline in inflation below the target rate of inflation. To maintain stable inflation, the central bank would then rely on a monetary expansion to avoid the recession. The converse would apply to a favorable demand shock. Fearing an increase in inflation above the target rate, the central bank would rely on a monetary contraction to slow the economy, and keep output at the natural level of output. As a result of this active monetary policy, output would remain at the natural level of output all the time

The result we have just derived - that inflation targeting eliminates deviations of output from its natural level - is too strong, however, for two reasons ;

1) The central bank cannot always achieve the rate of inflation it wants in the short run.

So suppose that, for example, the central bank was not able to achieve its desired rate of inflation last year, so π_{t-1} is higher than $\pi*$. Then it is not clear that the central bank should try to hit its target this year, and achieve $\pi_t=\pi^*$. The Phillips curve relation implies that such a decrease in inflation would require a potentially large increase in unemployment

2) Like all other macroeconomic relations, the Phillips curve relation above does not hold exactly. It will happen that, for example, inflation increases even when the unemployment is at the natural rate of unemployment. In this case, the central

bank will face a more difficult choice : whether to keep unemployment at the natural rate and allow inflation to increase, or to increase unemployment above the natural rate, to keep inflation in check.

These qualifications are important, but general point remain. Inflation targeting makes good sense in the medium run and allows for monetary policy to stabilize output around its natural level in the short run.

7. Interest Rate Rules.

The question is then how to achieve the inflation target. Inflation is crealy not under the direct control of the central bank. In answer to this question, John Taylor, from Stanford University, argued that, because the central bank affects spending through the interest rate, the central bank should think directly in terms of the choice of an interset rate rather than a rate of nominal money growth. He then suggested a rule that the central bank should follow to set the interest rate. This rule, which is now known as the Taylor rule, goes as follows :

1) Let π_t be the rate of inflation, and $\pi*$ be the target rate of inflation.

2) Let i_t be the nominal interest rate, and i^* be the target nominal interest rate-the nominal interest rate associated with

the target rate of inflation π^* in the medium run.

3) Let u_t be the unemployment rate, and u_n be the natural unemployment rate.

Think of the central bank as choosing the nominal interest rate, i. Then, Taylor argued, the central bank should follow the following rule :

$$i_t = i^* + a(\pi_t - \pi^*) - b(u_t - u_n)$$

where a and b are positive coefficents.

Let look at what the rule says :

◆ If inflation is equal to target inflation($\pi_t=\pi^*$), and the unemployment rate is equal to the natural rate of unemployment ($u_t=u_n$), then central bank should set the nominal interest rate i_t equal to its target value i^*. This way, the economy can stay on the same path, with inflation equal to the target inflation, and unemployment equal to the natural rate of unemployment.

◆ If inflation is higher than the target, the central bank should increase the nominal interest rate i_t above $i*$. This higher interest rate will increase unemployment, and this increase in unemployment will lead to a decrease in inflation

The coefficient a should, therefore, reflect how much the central bank cares about unemployment versus inflation. The higher a, the more the central bank will increase the interest rate in response to inflation, the more economy slow down, the more unemployment will increase, and the faster inflation will return to the target inflation rate.

In any case, Taylor pointed out, a should be larger than one. Why? Because what matters for spending is the real interest rate, not the nominal interest rate. When inflation increases, the central bank, if it wants to decrease spending and output, must increase the real interest rate. In other words, it must increase the nominal interest rate more than one for one with inflation.

◆ If unemployment is higher than the natural rate of unemployment, the central bank should decrease the nominal interest rate. The lower nominal interest rate will increase output, leading to a decrease in unemployment. Like the coefficient a, the coefficient b should reflect how much the central bank cares about unemployment relative to inflation. The higher b, the more the central bank will be willing to deviate from target inflation to keep unemployment close to the natural rate of unemployment.

In stating this rule, Taylor did not argue that it should be followed blindly. Many other events, such as an exchange rate crisis, or the need to change the composition of speding on goods, and thus the mix between monetary policy and fiscal policy, justify changing the nominal interest rate for other reasons than those included in the rule. But, he argued, the rule provided a useful way of thinking about monetary policy. Once the central bank has chosen a target rate of inflation, it should try to achieve it by adjusting the nominal interest rate. The rule it should follow should take into account not only current inflation but also current unemployment.

8. Disinflation and the Natural Rate Hypothesis

Our discussion of the cost of disinflation has been based on an assumption called the natural - rate hypothesis This is summarized in the following statement :

"Fluctuations in aggregate demand affect output and employment only in the short run. In the long run, the economy returns to the levels of output, employment, and unemployment described by the classical model."

The natural rate hypothesis allows macroeconomists to study seperately short run and long run developments in the economy. It is one expression of the classical dichotomy.

In the 1940s and 1950s, many Keynesian economists believed that expansionary fiscal policy could be used to achieve full employment on a permanent basis. In the 1960s. however, many economists realized that expansionary policy could cause problems with inflation, but they still believed policy makers could choose to trade off low unemployment for higher inflation even in the long run.

In 1968, however, Milton Friedman and Edmund Phelps of Columbia University, working independently, proposed the concept of the natural rate of unemployment. The natural rate unemployment is the nonaccelerating inflation rate of unemployment or NAIRU. According to the hypothesis of the NAIRU, inflation eventually gets built into expectation, so any attempt to keep the unemployment rate below the natural rate will lead to an ever-rising inflation rate.

The natural rate hypothesis gives a more limited role to activist macroecomic policy than did ealier ideas. Because the government can't keep unemployment below the natural rate, its task is not to keep unemployment low but to keep it stable to prevent large fluctuation in unemployment.

The important point to notice about the Friedman-Phelps hypothesis is that it made a strong prediction. Friedman and Phelps claimed that the apparent trade-off between unemployment and inflation would not survive an extended period of rising prices: once inflation was embodied in the public's expections, inflation would continue even in the face of high unemployment, Sure enough, that's exactly what happened in the 1970s. This successful prediction was one of the triumphs of macroeconomic analysis, and it convinced the great majority of economists that the natural rate hypothesis was correct. In contrast to traditional monetarism, the natural rate hypothesis has become almost universally accepted among macroecomists.

Recently, some economists have challenged the natural rate hypothesis by suggesting that aggregate demand may affect output and employment even in the long run, They have pointed out a number of machanisms through which recessions might leave permanent scars on the economy by altering the natural rate of unemployment. Hysteresis is the term used to describe the long lasting influence of history on the natural rate. In other words, a recession can raise the amount of frictional unemployment and the amount of structural unemployment.

Hysteresis remains a controversial theory. Some economists believe the theory helps explain persistently high unemployment in Europe, because the rise in European unemployment starting in th early 1980s coincided with disinflation but continued after inflation stabilized. Moreover, the increase in unemployment tended to be larger for those countries that experienced the greatest reductions in inflations, such as Ireland, Italy, and Spain. If it is true, the theory is important, because hysteresis greatly increases the cost of recessions. Put another way, histeresis raises the sarcifice ratio, because output is lost even after the period of disinflation is over.

<입증후 기록>

외국인의 자본이 유입되면 대부자금의 공급이 증가하기 때문에 이자율이 하락하고 투자지출이 증가하여 경제가 성장한다. 그런데 외국인의 자본이 어떤 이유에서 유출되기 시작하여 대폭적으로 유출되는 시기가 되면 (자본도피시에는) 외환시장에서 달러화의 부족으로 원·달러 환율이 급등하고 이자율이 상승하여 환율위기(exchange rate crisis) 또는 금융위기(financial crisis)에 빠질 수 있다. 이것이 2008년 우리 경제의 금융위기의 본질적인 내용이다. 이에 대해서는 미시경제와 거시경제적인 측면에서 접근해 보는 것이 보다 더 체계적이기 때문에 "경제이론과 현실" 연구방법론의 범위내에서 분석한 것을 <입증 후 기록>으로 첨부하였다.

1) 미시경제적 접근법

이론을 단순화하기 위해서 불확실성과 위험성이 존재하지 않기 때문에 외국인의 자본이 채권시장으로만 유입된다고 가정하자. 모든 것이 확실한 세계에서는 주식시장으로 유입되는 경우에도 그 경제적 효과는 채권시장으로 유입되는 경우와 같을 것이다. 그리고 채권시장으로 유입된다고 가정하고 이론이 전개되는 것이 일반적이다.

외국인의 자본이 유입되면 [그림21]에서 보는 바와 같이 이자율이 하락하고 투자지출이 증가하며, 생산성이 향상으로 경제성장에 기여한다. 이처럼 외국인의 자본이 우리 경제로 유입되었던 이유는 우리 경제의 투자 수익률과 이자율이 외국에 비해서 높았었기 때문이었다. 그런데 외환위기 이후 2000년대에 들어서면서 부터는 외국인의 투자자금이 대규모로 유입된 결과 이자율이 하락하여 2007년 8월까지 대체적으로 실질이자율은 미국의 실질이자율 보다도 낮은 수준이었다.

그림에서 보는 바와 같이, 외국인 투자가 증가하면 산출량이 EBCD 만큼 증가한다. 그 중 ABCD가 외국인 투자의 수익으로 외국인의 몫이기 때문에 외국인 투자로 인한 순편익은 EAD이다. 순편익은 자본·노동 비율의 증가로 인한 생산성의 향상으로 임금이 상승한다는 것을 뜻하는 것이다. 요약한다면 외국인의 자본의 유입으로 생산설비에 대한 투자가 증가하고, 그 결과 경제 성장에 기여하며, 따라서 외국인 투자 수익이 외국인에게 지급되는 이자와 배당을 초과한다는 것이다.

이것이 외국인투자를 순편익의 측면에서 분석한 것으로서 외국인 투자에 대한 미시경제적 일반론이라 할 수 있다.

[그림 21] 외국인 투자의 효과

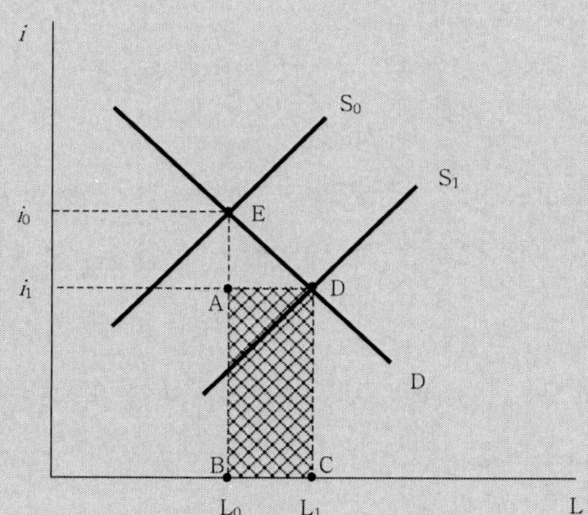

그런데 현실의 경제는 매우 불확실하기 때문에 1997년과 1998년 및 2003년도와 같이 주가는 폭락해서 저평가 될 수도 있고, 따라서 외국인의 자본이 주식시장으로만 유입될 수도 있다. 이자율이 하락하는 상태에서 외국인의 자본이 주식시장으로 유입되면 주식과 부동산 가격이 상승하고 원·달러환율이 하락한다. 이자율이 외국의 이자율보다 낮은 수준에서도 외국인의 자본이 주식시장으로의 유입이 지속된다면 원화의 가치가 과대평가될 수 있다. 예를 들면 외국인의 자본이 주식시장으로 유입된 결과 외국인의 지분이 40% 이상이나 되어 원·달러 환율은 2006년 5월 달러당 920원대까지 하락하였다.

이상의 설명에서 알 수 있는 바와 같이 이자율이 하락할 때 원·달러환율이 상승하지 않고 하락하는 이유는, 바꾸어 말한다면 거꾸로 가는 이유는, 우리 경제의 이자율이 외국의 이자율보다 낮은 상태에서도 외국인의 자본이 주식시장으로 유입되었기 때문이다. 결국 주가가 과대평가되는 수준까지 원·달러 환율은 하락하기 때문에 종합주가지수의 평가문제는 이자율과 배당뿐만 아니라 환율도 참고하는 것이 타당할 것으로 생각한다. 돌이켜볼때 원·달러환율이 900원대에서 종합주가지수 2000수준은 지금의 시점에서 보면 주가가 과대평가된 것이었다고 밖에 할 수 없을 것이다.

원화의 가치가 과대평가되거나 주가가 고평가되면 주식시장으로 유입되었던 외국인의 자본이 유출될 수 밖에 없는데 일시적으로 과도하게 유출되는 현상이 금융위기 또는 환율위기다. 따라서 금융위기는 2006년 5월부터 시작되었으나 주가가 상승하였기 때문에 잠재되어 있었다가 2007년 11월부터 나타나기 시작하여 2008년 11월까지 지속되었다. 2007년 11월 1일을 기준으로 한다면 원·달러환율은 그 후 1년동안 60%나 상승하였다.

그 이후 원·달러 환율이 달러당 1500원 이상으로 상승하지 않는 가장 중요한 이유는 원화의 가치가 폭락하여 더 이상 하락하지 않을 것으로 예상되기 때문이다.

2) 거시경제적 접근법

이론을 단순화하기 위해서 다음과 같은 가정하에서 출발하기로 하자.

(1) 외국인의 자본이 채권시장으로 유입되지 않고 주식시장으로만 유입되고 있다. 실제적으로도 외국인의 채권투자잔액은 외국인의 주식투자 잔액에 비해서 무시될 수 있을 정도로 낮은 수준이었다.

(2) 외국인 투자자들이 앞으로 외국인 자본이 유출되고, 원화의 가치가 하락(원·달러 환율의 상승)할 것이라고 예상한다. 바꾸어 말한다면 앞으로 1년후의 예상환율이 상승으로 현재의 환율도 상승한다는 가정이다. 실제적으로도 2007년 11월 1일부터 2008년 11월 현재까지 외국인의 자본의 유출로 주가는 하락하였고 원·달러환율은 달러당 900원 수준에서 1500원 수준까지 급등하였다.

(3) 외국인의 자본이 주식시장으로만 유입되기 때문에 국내주식투자수익률(r)과 외국의 주식투자수익률(r^*)이 다음과 같은 관계가 성립해야 외환시장이 균형을 이룬다.

$$r = r^* + \frac{E^e - E}{E}$$

여기에서 E^e는 원·달러의 예상환율이고, E는 현재의 환율이다. 이는 외환시장 균형조건인 이자율평가설(interest parity condition) 또는 이자율 평형설에서 채권투자수익률인 이자율(i) 대신에 주식투자수익률 r을 대입해 준 것에 지나지 않는다. 예를들어 원·달러의 예상환율(E^e)의 상승으로 앞으로 1년후에 원·달러환율이 30% 상승할 것이라고 예상한다면 한국의 연간 주가상승률이 외국의 주가상승률보다 30% 초과해야만 환율을 현재의 수준으로 유지할 수 있다는 것이다. 그렇지 않으면 외국인들이 국내주식을 팔고 그 대금으로 외환시장에서 달러화를 구입하게 된다. 따라서 달러화의 수요의 증가로 외환시장에서 달러화가 부족하게 되고 원·달러환율이 급등한다.

만약 중앙은행(한국은행)이 환율을 안정시키고자 한다면 외환시장에 개입해서 달러화를 팔고 원화를 구입해야하기 때문에 외환보유고가 감소한다.

실제적으로도 2008년도에는 한국은행이 환율을 안정시키고자한 결과 외환보유고가 대폭적으로 감소하였다. 극단적인 경우에는 외환보유고의 고갈로 1997년과 같은 외환위기에 빠질수도 있다.

이상의 설명에서 알 수 있는 것처럼 2008년도의 금융위기는 환율위기였다. 이미 설명한 바와 같이 환율위기는 2006년 5월부터 시작되었으나 주가가 상승하였기 때문에 잠재되어 있었다가 2007년 11월부터 본격적으로 나타나기 시작하여 2008년 10월과 11월에 절정을 이루었다. 그런데 문제를 복잡하게 만드는 것은 세계적인 금융위기로 인한 세계적인 경기침체 또는 국제적인 경기침체(international business cycles)로 앞으로 수출이 감소할 수 있기 때문이다.

외환위기 극복과정에서 알 수 있었던 바와 같이 단순한 금융위기인 경우에는 원·달러환율의 상승으로 순수출이 증가하면 위기를 극복할 수 있었지만 세계경제가 침체하면 수출이 감소하기 때문에 환율상승의 효과가 반감될 수 있다는 점이다. 바꾸어 말한다면 2008년도 까지는 수출이 지속적으로 증가되어 왔으나 앞으로는 수출이 둔화되어 감소할 수도 있다는 것이다. 만약에 수출이 장기적으로 감소한다면 지난 10년보다 앞으로 10년이 보다 더 어려운 상황이 전개될 수도 있다. 이와 같은 이유 때문에 2008년 12월부터는 확장적인 재정·금융정책이 적극적으로 검토되고 있다고 할 수 있다.

결국 우리경제는 두가지 문제에 직면하고 있는 것이 현실이다. 하나는 우리경제의 금융위기 또는 환율위기의 문제이고 또다른 하나는 세계적인 경기침체로 인한 경기침체의 문제이다. 세계적인 경기침체로 인한 경기침체의 문제는 "경제이론과 현실"의 연구방법과 범위를 벗어나는 문제이기 때문에 이 문제에 대한 논의는 여기에서는 더 이상 하지 않고 있다. 그리고 실제로 정책의 효과가 나타나는 시기도 2009년 6월 이후에나 있을 것으로 생각한다.

끝으로 1997년 외환위기 이후 2007년까지 우리경제의 연평균 물가상승률은 3.5% 내외였다. 그것도 환율을 달러당 900원까지 하락시킬 수 있었기 때문이었다. 바꾸어 말한다면 연간경제성장률이 5% 수준이 될 때마다 인플레이션 압력이 지속되었고, 인플레이션 압력이 지속될 때마다 원·달러환율을 하락시킬 수 있었기 때문에 연간물가상승률을 3.5% 수준으로 유지할 수 있었다고 할 수 있다. 그 후 2011년까지도 인플레이션 문제는 우리 경제의 매우 중요한 문제로 남아 있었다. 그런데 2015년 현재 우리 경제의 연간물가상승률은 1%내외로서 이제는 디플레이션이 우려되고 있다. 이처럼 물가의 안정은 우리경제의 가장 중요한 경제문제로 남아있다고 할 수 있다. 이와 같은 이유 때문에 입증자료의 말미에 "자연실업률의 측정상의 문제"를 "디스인플레이션과 자연률이론"으로 내용을 교체하여 이 책을 개정판으로 세트발행하고자 하였다.

INDEX

저 자 약 력

연세대학교 경영대학원(경제석사)

세종대학교 대학원 경제학과(경제박사수료)

세종대학교 경제학과 강사

현, 세계경제문제연구소

<경제이론과 현실> 완결편 **연구방법론**

2008년 12월 31일 초판 발행
2016년 3월 25일 개정판 발행

저 자 정 기 옥
발행인 정 기 옥
발행처 경제연구 출 판 세계경제문제연구소
서울시 강서구 등촌로 13다길 84 (화곡2동 866-23)
신고 2008. 7.10 / 제 2008-000018
전화 (02) 2681-9593
조판 POD나라 1800-1477

정가 13,000원